GLOBALIZATION at What Price?

Economic Change and Daily Life

Pamela K. Brubaker

THE
PILGRIM
PRESS
Cleveland

To Bob, with gratitude

The Pilgrim Press, 700 Prospect Avenue East, Cleveland, Ohio 44115-1100
pilgrimpress.com

© 2001 by Pamela Brubaker

All rights reserved. Published 2001

Printed in the United States of America on acid-free paper

06   05   04   5   4   3   2

Library of Congress Cataloging-in-Publication Data
Brubaker, Pamela, 1946-
    Globalization at what price? : economic change and daily life / Pamela K.
Brubaker.
        p.   cm.
    Includes bibliographical references and index.
    ISBN 0-8298-1438-8
    1. International economic relations. 2. International economic integration.
3. Globalization – Economic aspects. 4. Globalization – Social aspects.
5. Globalization – Environmental aspects. 6. Globalization – Moral and ethical
aspects. 7. Globalization – Religious aspects – Christianity. I. Title.

HF1359 .B77 2001
337 – dc21

                                                        2001036831

GLOBALIZATION
at What
Price?

Contents

Preface   7

Acronyms   13

1. Just What Is Globalization Anyway?   15

2. What Does Globalization Have to Do with Daily Life?   44

3. What Does Faith Have to Do with Globalization?   63

4. What Can I Do?   82

5. Can We Really Make a Difference?   100

Notes   121

Index   139

Preface

This book examines the ways that globalization affects our daily lives and the lives of others, the ethical questions that the global economy raises, and the resources that the Christian faith offers that equip people to work for economic justice. A recent full-page magazine advertisement for an executive management graduate program stated, "The Game Belongs to Those Who Prepare for It." A chessboard with a world map superimposed over it covers the ad. "Success in a global economy requires understanding, skill, and specialized knowledge," begins the ad copy. In its effort to interest prospective students in its program, this ad is premised on the astounding concept that the global economy is a game and the world is for the taking by the winners.[1] This is just advertising hyperbole, some might say. But there is a kind of truth to this claim.

According to the 1998 UN *Human Development Report,* the world's 225 richest people have a combined wealth of more than $1,000,000,000,000 ($1 trillion), which is equal to the annual income of the poorest 47 percent of the world's people. These are the biggest winners in the global economic game. The richest fifth of the world's people have also done well, increasing their share of the world's income from 70 percent in 1960 to 85 percent in 1991. During this same period the income share of the poorest fifth of the world's people dropped from 2.3 percent to 1.4 percent. These are the big losers, the 1.2 billion people—the majority of them women—that the World Bank reports live on less than $1 a day. This is a 20 percent increase since 1985, and the number of people in this group continues to increase. I am moved to ask, Globalization, at what price?

Behind these statistics are real people. I remember the poor women and children I met in Uganda as part of a World Council of Churches Women-to-Women Visit in the fall of 1998. The groups we visited were working at income-generating projects—sewing uniforms, spinning and weaving crafts—with the help of small loans from a Council fund. I particularly remember a woman seated outdoors on the ground, spinning yarn with a bicycle wheel turned into a spinning wheel, while her small children played nearby. One of the Ugandan fund officers we talked to admitted that these projects do not lift the women from poverty; rather, they keep them and their families from starvation. We passed by the largest factory in the country, a new Coca Cola bottling plant on the outskirts of the capital, Kampala. A forest had been cut down to build the plant. We were told that the people did not protest the cutting of the forest, because this was where dictator Idi Amin buried his victims. When I asked my host family what they thought of this plant, one member said that it did provide jobs with decent wages by local standards. Hellen Wangusa, of the African Women's Economic Policy Network, looked at it from a different perspective. Because of so-called economic reforms, poor women could no longer buy pineapple juice (grown in Uganda for export) for their children. Coca Cola is cheaper, but much less nutritious.

Or I think of the maquila I visited in the fall of 2000 with Borderlinks, a Tucson-based experiential education program.[2] A maquila is a foreign-owned factory whose workers assemble imported parts into products for export. Sitting along the Mexican side of the border, the maquila we visited makes electronics equipment (conductors and transformers). The workers there earn $4 a day (for a ten-hour day, six days a week), twice what many of the world's poor earn. Are they winners in the global economic game? Many have migrated from rural areas to these border cities because they can no longer scratch out a living on their small plots of land. The director of personnel admitted to us that $4 a day is not a living wage; she estimated that one person needed $10 to $12 a day to meet basic needs. (This maquila did provide free transportation and subsidize the cost of workers' lunches.) Our time in this area ended with a trip to a grocery, where we could see for ourselves the high cost of food: 1 gallon of milk cost 24 pesos, which meant 5 hours of work at the minimum wage (in the United States this would be the equivalent of $25 for a minimum-wage worker); 2 kg beans, 6.39 pesos or 1.3 hours of work (U.S.$6.65); 1 kg rice, 4 pesos or 50 minutes of work (U.S.$4.15); .5 kg beef, 23 pesos or 5 hours of work (U.S.$25). As we were leaving the maquila, we found out that its owner is a U.S. defense contractor whose headquarters are in California—not too far from where I live. What we were seeing, one of our group remarked, is "our tax dollars at work." Defense electronics is currently one of the most profitable industries. How much of that profit comes from contracting production out to low-wage countries?

The term *globalization* has been widely used for at least a decade. It was first used in the late 1960s or early 1970s to refer to "rapidly expanding political and economic interdependence," particularly between Western states. In their introduction to the globalization debate, David Held and Anthony McGrew define globalization as "the expanding scale, growing magnitude, speeding up and deepening impact of interregional flows and patterns of social interaction." They point out that the process of globalization is "deeply divisive" and "vigorously contested" because a significant portion of the world's population is largely excluded from its benefits.[3]

Two recent popular books are illustrative of the contested character of discussions about globalization and the "free market." Journalist Thomas Friedman, author of the best-selling *The Lexus and the Olive Tree: Understanding Globalization,* is a true believer in the benefits of globalization. He thinks that, since the fall of the Soviet Union, there is not nor will there be an alternative to free market capitalism. He asserts that "the spread of capitalism has raised living standards higher, faster and for more people than at any time in history." Friedman affirms the claim of Prince Talal of Saudi Arabia that "globalization is currently based on democracy, human rights, and market economics."[4]

In contrast, historian Thomas Frank, author of *One Market under God: Extreme Capitalism, Market Populism, and the End of Economic Democracy,* is skeptical of such claims. He describes the belief that the market is an expression of the will of the people as "market populism." Noting that the so-called New Economy "has exalted the rich and forgotten about the rest of us with a decisiveness that we haven't seen since the twenties," Frank writes that "market populism is, in many ways, the most blatant apologia for economic inequality since social Darwinism."[5]

My passion around these matters is rooted in my Christian faith and its call for justice. I first began to address the global economy after my participation in the UN Decade for Women Conference in Nairobi, Kenya, in 1985. I made connections between what I heard there about what was happening with women in Africa, Asia, and Latin America with experiences I had in the United States. From my experience and research, I determined that an adequate ethical analysis must include a feminist perspective.[6] My passion was rekindled by encounters with those who suffer greatly from unrestrained economic forces in the United States, particularly after my move to southern California in 1994, and recent trips to Mexico, Uganda, and Zimbabwe. These forces are undermining the livelihood of too many of the world's people, particularly the most vulnerable, and are contributing to serious ecological degradation.

Although globalization is impacting the lives of all, it is little understood by many people. Some have accepted the view articulated by former British prime minister Margaret Thatcher that "there is no alternative" to corporate-led global capitalism. At the same time, there is a sense of unease that at times erupts from beneath the surface (like the protests at the December 1999 World Trade Organization meeting in Seattle). Although few may take to the streets, many wonder about the income disparities and ecological damage that seem to result from globalization. Are there really no alternatives? Can we change the rules of the global economy to be more equitable and just?

This book is intended for people who want to better understand globalization, in hopes of envisioning a more just and equitable world. It explains key dynamics of corporate-led globalization and its impact on daily life. It examines ways that Christian faith can challenge the logic of this system and explores strategies for movements for economic justice. I intend it to be meaningful for people of faith—especially the chapter on faith and globalization—yet I hope that people of goodwill also will find it meaningful. This work is meant to be a contribution to ecumenical ethics, or what theologian Frederick Herzog calls "an ecumenical spirituality of discipleship," and also a contribution to what philosopher Roger Gottlieb calls a "spirituality of resistance."

I begin by presenting in chapter 1 an overview of globalization, what might be called a "primer." Drawing on the work of economists, sociologists, and activists, I describe key concepts and dynamics such as the globalization of capital, markets, and labor; economic restructuring; and privatization—this in language that nonspecialists can understand. I situate globalization historically, with a focus on the post–World War II period during which key institutions such as the World Bank, the International Monetary Fund, and the forerunner to the World Trade Organization developed. I conclude this overview with a brief examination of the harmful effects of globalization on people and the environment.

In chapter 2, I explore issues such as global food production and sweatshops, since food and clothing are products in our daily lives that integrate us into the global economy.[7] They are useful examples of the intersections of unjust gender, racial/ethnic, and class systems within and between nations. They also point to the need for systemic transformation of the political economy for justice to prevail. My primary purpose in the first part of the book is to relate globalization to the daily lives of people of some privilege, to help make the connections, identify the actors, and challenge the taken-for-granted character of globalization.

Since I write as a Christian ethicist, my work is grounded in the call of our faith to love of neighbor, solidarity with the poor and oppressed. I recently learned that delegates from developing nations to an international conference on missiology asked, "Why are the North American churches so silent about the evils of global capitalism?" Chapter 3 attempts to address that question. I explore the resources that scripture and religious tradition, when interpreted through a feminist liberation lens, offer for the development of critical voice and vision in relation to forces of economic globalization.

In chapters 4 and 5, I examine some ways that individuals and faith communities in alliance with secular justice movements can address issues of economic justice, particularly those discussed in the first part of the book. The purpose of this section is not only to provide information about specific strategies and campaigns, but also to develop awareness that the situation is not hopeless. We may feel caught in the midst of forces beyond our control, but from that position we can push for social justice in ways that make a difference in people's lives.

This book grew out of many experiences, but three are particularly significant. First is the 1985 UN Decade for Women Conference and the Non-governmental Organization Forum in Nairobi, Kenya. It was in the Forum workshops and the meetings with Nairobi area women's groups that the harmful effects of globalization first became real to me. A 1998 trip to Uganda as part of the World Council of Churches Women-to-Women Visits deepened this awareness, as did participation in the End of the Ecumenical Decade of the Churches in Solidarity with Women Celebration in Harare, Zimbabwe. Intense conversations with my traveling companions Ada María Isasi-Díaz and Hyung Kyung Chung added significantly to my learnings. I thank Sisterfund for helping support our participation in these Council events.

Most recent was a trip to the U.S.-Mexican border with the Tucson-based Borderlinks experiential education program, which brought to life the impacts of the North American Free Trade Agreement. This event was sponsored by the Sweatshop Action Committee of the Mobilization for the Human Family, a prophetic community in greater Los Angeles. I have learned much from my work with this organization about globalization, coalition building, and solidarity.

California Lutheran University has provided support for my research, travel to Africa, and a sabbatical leave in the fall of 2000. California Lutheran also made it possible for me to participate in the first class of the Lutheran Academy of Scholars (funded by a grant from Lutheran Brotherhood). Much of chapter 3 took shape in this year-long seminar.

I am grateful to Pilgrim Press's Timothy Staveteig, for his encouragement to write a book on this topic, and George Graham, for his enthusiasm to bring the project to completion.

Marilyn Legge, Sarah Forth, and Bob Weissman—colleagues and friends—offered invaluable suggestions after reading sections of my manuscript. I am deeply grateful for their encouragement and careful eyes. I continue to be indebted to my children, John Lowe and Cory Lowe, and to my extended family for their ongoing love and encouragement.

Acronyms

AIP	Apparel Industry Partnership
APALC	Asian Pacific American Legal Center
BIP	Border Industrialization Program
FDI	foreign direct investment
FLA	Fair Labor Association
FPEI	foreign portfolio equity investments
FTAA	Free Trade Area of the Americas
GATT	General Agreement on Tariffs and Trade
GDP	gross domestic product
GNP	gross national product
HIPC	highly indebted poor country
HRW	Human Rights Watch
IFDP	Institute for Food and Development Policy
IFPRI	International Food Policy Research Institute
IMF	International Monetary Fund
MAI	Multilateral Agreement on Investments
NAFTA	North American Free Trade Agreement
NCDM	National Commission on Democracy in Mexico
NLC	National Labor Committee
OECD	Organization for Economic Cooperation and Development

PRSP	Poverty Reduction Strategy Paper
SAL	structural adjustment loan
SAP	structural adjustment program
TNC	transnational corporation
TRIM	Trade-Related Investment Measures
TRIP	Trade-Related Intellectual Property Rights
UFW	United Farm Workers
UNCTAD	United Nations Commission on Trade and Development
UNDP	United Nations Development Program
UNICEF	United Nations Children's Fund
UNITE	Union of Needletrades, Industrial and Textile Employees
USAID	United States Agency for International Development
USAS	United Students Against Sweatshops
WCC	World Council of Churches
WHD	Wage and Hour Division
WRC	Worker Rights Consortium
WTO	World Trade Organization

ONE

Just What Is Globalization Anyway?

Globalization is a two-edged sword, bringing benefits to some and
misery to others.

— ROB VAN DRIMMELEN,
World Council of Churches Development Officer, 1998

The rich and middle classes are enjoying increasing variety and availability of consumer goods produced to the standards of the global
market, while the poor have to fight for their daily bread, primary
education and basic health facilities.

— MARGARET KALAISELVI,
Tamil Nadu Theological Seminary Professor, India, 1998

Throughout much of the developing world, globalization is seen, not
as a term describing objective reality, but as an ideology of predatory
capitalism. Whatever reality there is in this view, the perception of a
siege is unmistakable. Millions of people are suffering; savings have
been decimated; decades of hard-won progress in the fight against
poverty are imperiled.

— KOFI ANNAN, UN Secretary-General,
at Harvard University, 1998

Many Americans are becoming increasingly aware of globalization.
Our lives and communities are being changed by its impact. The
place where I grew up, Preble County in southwestern Ohio, is a rural county of about forty thousand people. When I was child, in the
1950s, there was hardly any manufacturing industry in the county.
Most residents who were not family farmers commuted to blue-
collar jobs in neighboring counties, which had industrialized cities.
Our county was home to a homogenous population of WASPs;
neighboring counties had sizeable African American and Catholic
populations. Today, the few family farms that remain look, as do the

15

corporate farms, to increasing exports to Asia and other regions for their survival. Economic turmoil there can wreak havoc here. Many farmers in the county shared the same concern as Charles Burrus, an Illinois hog farmer, who was worried about losing his six-hundred-acre farm. Because of the Asian economic crisis, his loss on a semi load of hogs was $10,000 to $15,000. His hogs, like those of many other U.S. farmers, had been exported to Asia at a profit, but, with currency devaluation and economic hard times, this market dried up. "We've never seen this heavy a loss in the pork industry, not even in the Depression."[1]

Changes in the local economy and culture include a small factory established in the county seat in the 1970s moving to Mexico. Several undocumented Mexicans working in a nearby county were recently arrested in an INS raid. A Japanese consortium owns the steel mill in another neighboring county. Growing numbers of medical specialists in nearby counties (our county still does not have a hospital) have emigrated from India and other Asian countries. A large mosque was built in another neighboring county to serve the area's growing Muslim population.

This reality is described by Ulrich Beck as "globality," which means "*we have been living for a long time in a world society,* in the sense that the notion of closed spaces has become illusory." (To paraphrase Beck, not even a rural Midwestern county like the one I come from is cut off from other places.) Beck distinguishes globality (and globalization) from *globalism,* which is "the ideology of rule by the world market, or the ideology of neoliberalism." Beck contends that globality is irreversible. He gives several reasons to support this claim, which we can comprehend from our own experience. For instance, there is the "ongoing revolution of information and communications technology," something most of us understand from the impact of computers and the Internet on our lives. We also have some awareness of the expansion and greater density of international trade when we notice where the products we purchase are made. From news reports if not personal experience, we know that finance markets are networked globally, that the power of transnational corporations is increasing, and that there are more transnational actors, such as the World Trade Organization, in world politics. We are increasingly exposed "to the stream of images from the global culture industries," ranging from world music to the success of a film like *Crouching Tiger, Hidden Dragon.*[2]

It is apparent that globalization has many facets: economic, political, cultural, and social. This book focuses primarily on economic aspects of globalization, particularly what some call "the global economy." However, since I am focusing on the rules of the globalization game and who has the power to make them, the political aspect cannot be ignored. Thus, I am doing a political-economic analysis. In the first section of this chapter I present an overview of globalization. Key concepts will be defined and significant actors and dynamics in the globalization process identified. The second section is a brief history of globalization, with a focus on two key turning points since World War II—first, the 1944 Bretton Woods conference, and then, the 1980s triumph of the neoliberal agenda. Finally, we will need to ask some crucial questions, such as "Who gains and who loses from this process?"[3] Thus, the third section examines some of the effects of globalization on people and the environment. In other words, *globalization at what price?*

An Overview of the Global Economy

The Field Guide to the Global Economy offers a straightforward definition of economic globalization as "the flows of goods and services, capital, and people across national borders."[4] Factors contributing "to the emergence of a single global market for capital, goods, and services" are a decrease in the cost of transportation and communication, as well as reduction of import tariffs, quotas, and foreign exchange controls.[5] Thomas Friedman contends that globalization is "largely a technology-driven phenomenon," with the development of communication, transportation, and computer technology inevitably and naturally leading to globalization.[6] But Peter Marcuse cautions that developments in technology and developments in the concentration of power, "often lumped together under the rubric of globalization," are distinct. Furthermore, he asserts that "the link between advances in technology and the concentration of economic power is not an inevitable one."[7] Rather, it is changes in the rules that enable this concentration.

It is important to remember that goods and services, capital and people, have all moved across national borders for centuries. One could point to ancient traders like the Phoenicians, Chinese, and Arabs, conquests like those of Alexander the Great or the Crusades, and the global colonization arising from the European conquest of the Americas, Asia, and Africa. "Present-day globalization differs from these earlier processes," according to van Drimmelen, "both in nature (its emphasis on liberalization and deregulation) and in scope and intensity."[8]

The nature of present-day globalization is capitalist. What is particularly distinctive about capitalism is its focus on profit seeking and the accumulation of capital and the private ownership of the means of production. The term "capital" was not in use before the 1600s. It refers to that factor of production—"tools, equipment, factories, raw materials, goods in process, means of transporting goods, and money"—that is used for production for profit. A share of profit is then devoted to the production of other goods, and the process is repeated over and over, resulting in the accumulation of more and more capital.[9] Classical economists like Adam Smith and David Ricardo believed that "free trade"—not controlled by the state or tradition—leads to the most efficient use of land, labor, and capital. Present-day neoclassical economists ground their support of capitalist globalization in this view.[10] The understanding of capitalism that is put forth in this work is informed by Beverly Wildung Harrison, who writes, "What is distinctive about capitalism is neither unrestricted markets nor the existence of private property, per se. Rather, its distinctive feature is the private control of the *means of production*—resources, machines, and other people's labor."[11]

Goods and Services

Some data will sketch in the changes in scope and intensity of present-day globalization. In the one-hundred-year period from 1870 to 1973, the percentage of world output of goods and services that were exports grew from 5 percent of the total to 12 percent. Then in just over two decades—from 1973 to 1996—it nearly doubled, now accounting for 23.6 percent of total production. (As we examine the types of goods and services that are traded, readers might want to think about their own purchasing patterns.) Of the goods traded across borders, the largest segment is made up of cars, trucks, and car parts (8.6 percent), followed by textiles, footwear, and clothing (7.8 percent), and petroleum products (6.9 percent); these three segments alone account for close to one-fourth of the total. In regard to trade in services, growth has occurred in tourism and travel, communications, advertising, entertainment, and legal services. The export of services accounts for over one-fourth of U.S. total exports, but only 15 percent for the world's exports.[12]

Illegal trade, often organized by criminal syndicates and cartels, is also considerable. Since this trade is illegal, only an estimate of its value is available. Illicit drugs amount to perhaps 8 percent of total international trade. Smuggling of endangered animals amounts to about $5 billion annually. There is also an illegal trade in people, sometimes called trafficking. The United Nations estimates that four million people a year fall victim to traffickers for about $7 billion in profits. These figures include both international and internal trafficking, such as the forced migration of women from rural areas to work in urban sex industries. There are no reliable estimates of the illegal trade in weapons. A total of $111 billion was spent on "legal" international trade in armaments between 1995 and 1999. The United States has supplied weapons for forty-five of the fifty conflicts raging in the last decade—$42 billion worth. This trade may be profitable for CEOs and stockholders, but it exacerbates conflicts, some of which have their roots in the growing inequality produced by economic globalization.[13]

Economist Peter Dicken asserts that up until about three decades ago, international economic integration was "shallow," exhibited mainly in "arm's length trade in goods and services between independent firms and through international movements of portfolio capital." In contrast, economic integration is now "deep," "organized primarily by transnational corporations" and extending to "the level of production of goods and services." Transnational corporations (TNCs) are key actors in the present form of globalization, enough so that some call this form corporate globalization. Dicken offers a useful definition of a TNC as "a firm which has the power to co-ordinate and control operations in more than one country, even if it does not own them." He refers to this process of coordination and control as "a spider's web of collaborative relationships," or "production chains." These are either producer or buyer driven.

"Producer-driven chains" are characterized by strong control of the process from the TNC's administrative headquarters. Examples include the automotive and computer industry. In "buyer-driven chains," retailers, brand-name merchandisers, or trading companies play the crucial role in setting up decentralized production networks in many different exporting countries. Examples include the apparel and shoe industries.[14]

According to the United Nations, the number of TNCs has grown from around 7,000 in 1970 to some 44,000 in 1998, a sixfold increase in less than three decades. In addition to 280,000 affiliates, TNCs operate through hundreds of thousands of links, which include subcontracts, licensing agreements, and strategic alliances between parent companies and other entities. Nike would be a prime example of this approach.[15] Van Drimmelen points out, "In 1970 a typical large US company earned 10–20 percent of its income from abroad; now many earn at least half their profits outside the US."[16]

Two-thirds of the world trade in goods and services is accounted for by TNCs. As much as one-third of this trade consists of transactions taking place within an individual TNC. In other words, parts are sent from one country to another country for assembly (which counts as an export for the sending country, an import for the receiving one), and then the assembled part is returned for sale (now counting as an import for the country that originally sent out the parts). Van Drimmelen notes that there is colossal secrecy about the way in which these "internal transfer prices are established and used," because this is an excellent way to minimize taxation. "Even governments often regard such matters as internal to the TNC." It is estimated that all this TNC activity—two-thirds of world trade—accounts for just 5 percent of the world's employment. However, TNCs control about one-third of the world's productive assets (capital). They generate about half of the greenhouse gas emissions, which contribute to global warming. Mining and commercial logging by some TNCs play a part in deforestation.[17]

Just two hundred of these forty thousand or so TNCs dominate global economic activity. Between 1983 and 1997, the growth in world gross domestic product was 144 percent; the sales of the top two hundred TNCs grew 160 percent, while their profits grew

224 percent.[18] The world's five hundred largest corporations saw similar growth during roughly the same period; their sales increased by 140 percent, their assets by 230 percent, and compensation for their corporate executive officers by 610 percent.[19] Of the top one hundred economies in the world, only forty-nine are countries; fifty-one are corporations.[20] From this arises the concern of some that the concentration of economic power threatens the sovereignty of nation-states—a topic we will explore later.

Capital

The second type of increased cross-border flow is capital. Like goods and services, capital also has flowed across borders for centuries, but its flow has also changed in scope and intensity. To follow this, it is most useful to look at financial flows. Finance refers to the system that incorporates the circulation of money, the granting of credit, the making of investments, and the provision of banking facilities. Individuals, banks, corporations, and other institutions such as pension funds all participate in cross-border financial transactions. Since 1980, these financial flows have increased rapidly, much faster than the increase in trade of goods and services. This increase is made possible, in large part, by liberalization of governmental regulations—a change in the rules—making foreign investment easier.

One form of cross-border financial flow is foreign direct investment (FDI). This usually takes the form of a corporation—a TNC—establishing or purchasing a lasting interest in, and degree of influence over, the management of a business in another country. In 1995, the value of FDI controlled by TNCs reached $2.7 trillion.[21] FDI involves bundling together financial capital and technology, as well as other strategic inputs. According to Susan George, in any one year as much of two-thirds to three-quarters of FDI "is not devoted to new, job-creating investment but to Mergers and Acquisitions which almost invariably result in job losses."[22] "Since 1983, foreign direct investments have grown five times faster than world trade and ten times faster than world output."[23]

A second type of financial flow is foreign portfolio equity investments (FPEI), the cross-border purchase of stocks and bonds, or the deposit of funds in foreign banks. Financial institutions and investors like pension funds or investment trusts usually make these transactions. Investors from industrialized countries increased their spending on "overseas stocks" by almost two hundred times between 1970 and 1997.[24] FPEI is less dependable than FDI, because portfolio investors are interested only in a good return on their investment, and there usually is no long-term commitment.

The third principal type of cross-border financial flow is debt flows (loans or bonds). Both public and private institutions make loans. The banking industry is even more concentrated than TNCs. By 1997, the top one hundred banks had combined assets of $21.3 trillion, an amount equal to almost three-fourths of annual global economic activity. Private debt flows to developing countries increased from under $20 billion in 1990 to $100 billion in 1997—a fivefold increase. The total debt owed by all developing countries exceeds $2 trillion dollars.[25] The debt crisis of some of these countries will be discussed in the next section.

Thus, it is evident that a lot of capital is crossing borders. Although most of these flows are between industrialized countries, there has been an increase in the share of foreign investment going to developing countries. For instance, between 1990 and 1996, the share of investment going to developing countries increased from 20 percent of the total to 34 percent. However, these flows are concentrated, with three-fourths of private financial flows (primarily from TNCs) going to just ten countries. In 1996, China alone received more than $52 billion, Mexico $28 billion. The hundred poorest countries, with one-fifth of the world's population, receive only 1 percent. Or put another way, 28 percent of the world's population—those in the "developed" and the ten "most important developing" countries—receives 91.5 percent of the FDI.[26]

Some readers may be wondering about foreign aid to developing countries. Over the past ten to fifteen years, there has been a decline in what is called overseas development aid—financial flows from richer to developing countries. (As we have seen, at the same time there has been an increase in private capital in the form of foreign direct investment and portfolio investment, with the expectation of profit making.) Foreign aid accounts for less that 1 percent of the U.S. budget and just one-fourth of 1 percent of its total gross national product (GNP). Furthermore, almost three-fourths of this aid is actually spent in the United States. A lot of government foreign aid goes to benefit transnational corporations by opening new markets and expanding foreign trade, or for militarization of developing countries, which benefits weapons manufacturers but exacerbates conflicts in various regions. The U.S. fiscal 1999 international affairs budget was just over $20 billion, which covers state department operating expenses as well as foreign aid. At least 10 percent of this total goes to cash transfers to Israel and Egypt. Sustainable-development activities that would benefit women and children total only $1.7 billion. Contrast this to over $6 billion for military aid. Globally, official development assistance to low-income and least-developed countries fell by U.S.$3.6 billion in 1997 from the prior year. An independent review of this aid concluded that "the world's poorest countries—with an average income of less than $2 a day—are getting lamentably low percentages of reduced aid."[27]

Cross-border speculation in currency, stocks, and bonds has become a lucrative source of wealth—at least for the winners. This phenomenon began on a large scale in the 1970s and 1980s after a long absence, due to the loosening of capital controls that had been imposed during the Great Depression. These controls limited the right of companies and citizens to buy foreign securities or invest overseas and limited to small amounts how much foreign currency people could buy.[28] This renewed speculative activity has been dubbed "the casino economy," which seems an appropriate term in that this activity consists of betting on whether these assets will go up or down in value. The growth in currency speculation is astounding. Between 1986 and 1998, the amount of average daily global trading of currencies grew from $200 billion to $1.6 trillion—an eightfold increase in little more than a decade. This dwarfs the trade in goods and services. According to economist David Korten, "The $1 trillion that changes hands each day in the world's international currency markets is itself 20 to 30 times the amount required to cover daily trade in actual goods and services."[29] Robert Reich, former secretary of labor in the Clinton administration, observes, "The set of symbols developed to represent real assets has lost the link with any actual productive activity. Finance has progressively evolved into a sector all its own, only loosely connected to industry."[30]

The data in this section documents enormous increases in the scope and intensity of cross-border flows of goods, services, and capital. Scholars offer various theories as to the significance of this phenomenon, yet nearly all agree on a few key points. First is a recognition of an increase in economic connections both within and among regions. Second is an awareness that new inequalities of wealth, power, privilege, and knowledge are being created, while at the same time traditional hierarchies are being challenged. Third is the realization that the development of cross-border problems, like global warming or the spread of HIV/AIDS, calls into question the role of national governments. At the same time, there is a growth of international governing institutions that raises crucial questions about the kind of world order being created and whose interests are being served by it. Finally, there is agreement on a need for new modes of thinking about and imaginative responses to these changes.[31] In order to develop these ways of thinking and responses, we need an understanding of how the current situation came about. Who are the key actors? What were turning points?

A Brief History of Globalization

As I indicated earlier, economic globalization is not a new phenomenon. Of course, none of the prior cross-border movements began to be truly global until after the 1492 European conquest of the Americas. Some theorists argue that the "belle époque" of globalization was the period just prior to World War I, from 1890 to 1914. However, the institutions that play a key role in the current period—that set the rules of the global game—were established toward the end of World War II. It is at this point that we begin our story.

Bretton Woods

In July of 1944, the UN Monetary and Financial Conference was held at Bretton Woods, New Hampshire. The purpose of this conference, according to Henry Morgenthau, U.S. secretary of the treasury and president of the conference, was "the creation of a dynamic world economy in which the peoples of every nation will be able to realize their potentialities in peace and enjoy increasingly the fruits of material progress on an earth infinitely blessed with natural resources."[32]

Three institutions were created at Bretton Woods that led the postwar push to globalize the world's economies. These were the World Bank, the International Monetary Fund (IMF), and the General Agreement on Tariffs and Trade (GATT). The World Bank, organized as the International Bank for Reconstruction and Development, was to provide capital for the reconstruction and development of war-torn nations. After Europe and Japan were rebuilt, the Bank focused on developing the countries in the southern hemisphere. This was to be accomplished by borrowing money from capital markets in the northern hemisphere to lend at a profit to countries in the south. The conditions for borrowing eventually came to include national economic and financial policies. The IMF was to promote cooperation "on monetary policies, exchange rate stability and the expansion of world trade." Its approach was to help countries that had a short-term balance of payment problems so that they would not need to devalue their currency, impose exchange rate controls, or cut back on imports from other countries.

An International Trade Organization was proposed at Bretton Woods. However, its creation was blocked by the U.S. Congress, which thought it would harm U.S. interests. (It was seen as too friendly to labor and "third world" countries.) The General Agreement on Tariffs and Trade (GATT) was organized in its place. GATT was a framework for ongoing negotiations on reduction in tariffs to expand trade. During the fifty years between 1947 and 1997, tariffs dropped from almost 40 percent to around 4 percent, which greatly stimulated the process of globalization. After successive rounds of GATT, the World Trade Organization (WTO) was established in 1995 as the institution responsible for setting and enforcing the rules of trade.[33]

WTO jurisdiction was expanded to include Trade-Related Investment Measures (TRIMs), the elimination of barriers to the system of internal cross-border trade of product components among TNCs, and Trade-Related Intellectual Property Rights (TRIPs), which set enforceable global rules on patents, copyrights, and trademarks (like pharmaceuticals). A particularly egregious example is Gerber Products' campaign against a 1983 Guatemalan law that forbids makers of baby formula to claim that their products (rather than mother's milk) are necessary for healthy babies. The law was recommended by the World Health Organization and had contributed to significant reductions in infant mortality since its passage. Gerber claimed that this law violated their trademark, a picture of a healthy baby. Rather than face a trade challenge, in 1995 Guatemala amended the law to exempt imported baby food products. Particularly troubling is the WTO's unprecedented dispute resolution system. Unlike GATT, WTO rulings are automatically binding and do not require unanimous consent to be adopted. All dispute panel meetings are closed, and their activities and documents confidential. There is no protection of due process, nor is citizen participation permitted.[34]

In the World Bank and the IMF, voting power is related to money: the more money a country contributes, the more votes it has. The WTO, like the United Nations, is based on a one-country, one-vote system. But critics charge that even the WTO and the United Nations are dominated by the power of large industrialized countries that control the World Bank and IMF.

Given the original goals of these institutions—reconstruction and trade expansion—one could conclude that they have been successful. Rob van Drimmelen notes that the decades between 1948 and 1971 "were a time without parallel in the economic history of the world." During this period world industrial production grew by 5.6 percent a year, and trade expanded even faster. Although the benefits of this growth were unequally distributed, "it was significantly less unfavourable to poor people and poor countries than the ensuing period has been."[35] What has changed?

Although the historical factors involved in these changes are complex, the ending of fixed exchange rates had significant implications. Fixed exchange rates were the foundation of the Bretton Woods system. The value of national currencies was expressed in gold or in U.S. dollars, which could be exchanged at a fixed price into gold. President Richard Nixon ended the dollar's link to gold in 1973. Other large economies shifted to floating exchange rates, which helped create the conditions for the currency speculation described above. This move lessened the ability of governments, which were presumed to be crucial actors within this system, to control international money and capital flows.

This then required a shift in the responsibilities of the IMF and World Bank. The IMF no longer needed to supervise the fixed exchange rate system for currencies. Instead, it directed its attention to providing funds to countries in distress (thus it is sometimes referred to as "the bank of last resort"), first in the south, then eastern Europe and the former Soviet Union. As previously indicated, the World Bank also turned its attention to the south and expanded its lending beyond specific projects. Both institutions attached conditions for the loans they made, which have had devastating impacts on many countries, as I will show in the last section of the chapter.

Neoliberalism

According to economist Susan George, neoliberalism came to ascendancy in the late 1970s through the work of a "highly efficient ideological cadre" based on the work of University of Chicago philosopher-economist Friedrich von Hayek, and students of his, like Milton Friedman. Neoliberalism builds on the work of classical economists like Adam Smith, David Ricardo, and John Stuart Mill, who advocated the end of government intervention in economic matters, such as restrictions on manufacturing or barriers to trade such as tariffs—in other words, deregulation and liberalization. They believed that free trade was the most effective path to economic growth. During the Great Depression of the 1930s, economist John Maynard Keynes asserted that "full employment is necessary for capitalism to grow and it can be achieved only if governments and central banks intervene to increase employment." Keynes's philosophy influenced President Roosevelt's formation of the "New Deal."

The central value of neoliberalism is competition, which is best expressed through the "free market." The ideas and policies in the "standard neoliberal toolkit" have to do with the market, the state, corporations, unions, and citizens. The market is to make major social and political decisions. The state should voluntarily reduce its role in the economy. Corporations are to have complete freedom. Unions are to be restrained and citizens given much less rather than more social protection. One of the greatest achievements of neoliberalism's proponents is that "they have made neo-liberalism seem as if it were the natural and normal condition of humankind."[36] Margaret Thatcher had been influenced by neoliberalism, and when she became prime minister of Great Britain in 1979, she instituted a neoliberal program that she called TINA—There Is No Alternative. Ronald Reagan, elected to the U.S. presidency a year later, began the neoliberal transformation of the U.S. economy.

Sociologist Walden Bello asserts that "the Reagan administration came to power with an agenda to discipline the Third World." This was part of a "roll back" policy—"on the international front, rolling back communism from Eastern Europe, China, and eventually the Soviet Union, and, in the domestic arena, rolling back 'big government' and 'big labor' from domestic economic life." Bello cites documents from the Heritage Foundation, a right-wing think tank that was influential during the Reagan-Bush years. The Foundation believed that the southern countries (through the Group of 77, an organization of less-developed countries which grew from 77 to 127 states acting together on their interests) had for a decade been attempting to undermine the north. The Foundation wrote, "At the Algiers nonaligned summit of 1973, the Group of 77 urged political unity to gain economic power. The participants demanded economic concessions by Western nations. The following year they moved their campaign to the UN General Assembly, and approved the 'Declaration on Establishment of a New International Economic Order' (NIEO) and the 'Charter of Economic Rights and Duties of States.' " The Heritage Foundation opposed the efforts of the south to create a new international economic order through international treaties, regulation of transnational trade and production, and a fairer redistribution of wealth, income, and technology.[37]

What developed to counter the call for a new international economic order is called the Washington Consensus. (In addition to the Washington Consensus there are the Human Development Consensus, represented by UNICEF and the UN Development Program, and the People-Centered Consensus.) This is the combination of policy prescriptions consistently advocated by the U.S. Treasury Department and the IMF: liberalization, deregulation, and privatization, packaged together in structural adjustment programs (SAPs) with an emphasis on export-led growth as conditions of IMF and World Bank loans. Deregulation refers to the withdrawal of the state from providing control or oversight over economic and financial transactions, the elimination of any government interventions that could affect the free functioning of the market—such as price controls or public subsidies. Privatization involves the transfer of ownership and management of public enterprises to private companies, which gives the private sector a larger role in providing all types of goods and services. Liberalization means lowering or removing tariffs, duties, and the like; giving up any domestic control over essential sectors such as trade and finance; allowing foreign companies to own key enterprises such as national banks, letting up on controls on foreign investment and capital.[38] Thomas Friedman calls these free market rules the Golden Straitjacket. "Those countries that put on the Golden Straitjacket and keep it on are rewarded by the herd with investment capital to grow. Those that don't put it on are disciplined by the herd—either by the herd avoiding that country or withdrawing its money from that country."[39]

One might think that these policy prescriptions were based on some empirical analysis, but that was not always the case. Joseph Stiglitz, former chief economist of the World Bank, writes, "There never was economic evidence in favor of capital market liberalization. There still isn't. It increases risk and doesn't increase growth." He thought that there would have been an "intellectual basis... required for a major change in international rules." He found that there was not. "It was all based on ideology"—neoliberalism.[40] As I will show in the next section, these prescriptions have had a devastating impact on people around the world.

In place of the economic development policies advocated by the Group of 77, "the neo-liberal school of economics questioned the usefulness of explicit development policies altogether and gave rise to a liberal and free market style of development," according to the authors of *Women, the Environment and Sustainable Development*.[41] Crucial processes included the globalization of production, primarily by TNCs, and increased dependence, particularly by developing countries, on export-led economic growth. Free trade zones—also called export processing zones—are a primary form that these processes took.

Export Processing Zones

At the end of the twentieth century, there were over one hundred export processing zones in fifty-one countries, which produce manufactured goods for export. These zones are set-aside areas within a country, with relaxed environmental and labor regulations and reduced taxes and tariffs. "The preferred labor force in these zones is female, very young, and with little or no previous work experience." Most of these women are migrants from rural areas of the country, which are called "supporting agricultural regions." Countries establish these zones to improve their international economic position and to get hard currency for debt servicing. Although these zones were supposedly dedicated to free trade, states would give subsidies to the industries in these zones and "ensure labor tranquility through repressive tactics."[42] In some cases, these zones were the forerunners to development of free trade areas. This meant that the zones were no longer limited to certain areas of the country. Instead, the entire country became a free trade zone.

Mexico is a good example of this, moving from free trade zones along the U.S.-Mexican border region to now being a part of the North American Free Trade Agreement. In the mid-1960s, Mexico passed the Border Industrialization Program (BIP, or maquiladora), which "encouraged foreign industrial investment through the use of government subsidies and new regulations that granted manufacturers duty-free importation of machinery, parts, and raw material." A primary purpose of this program was "to provide employment for seasonal migrant laborers (almost all of whom were male) who had lost their livelihood" when the United States ended the Bracero Program in 1964. Under the provisions of this program, which started in 1942, Mexican migrants had been able to come to the United States to work after being "officially assigned to agricultural and railroad construction jobs" there. BIP soon became a national strategy, as "an array of new state policies established a new factory regime based on a less organized, lower-paid, female workforce in new cities and regions."[43] The National Council of the Maquiladora Industry estimates that it will generate over $15 billion worth of value-added production in 2000, a 16 percent increase from 1999. The Mexican government expects to collect $482.8 million from maquiladora companies as taxes in 2000, which is "less than half a percent of all public revenue [taxes and fees], even though the companies account for about 3.5 percent of gross domestic product (GDP)."[44]

Mexico adopted the neoliberal model in the mid-1980s, in hopes of pulling the country out of significant international debt. William Greider writes that this involved "mass privatization by selling off the state-owned industrial groups to private investors both in Mexico and abroad, deregulating financial markets and shrinking the government's subsidies and controls in commerce, relaxing the various trade barriers that protected domestic producers and signing the GATT treaty." NAFTA only speeded up what was already underway. A crucial difference, though, was that as a precondition for entry into NAFTA, the Mexican Constitution had to be changed so that indigenous peoples lost their communal land rights.[45] These changes have had a devastating impact on the majority of Mexico's people.

Effects of Globalization on People and the Environment

Now that I have presented an overview of economic globalization, it is time to turn to the question "Who gains and who loses from this process?" In his discussion of the Bretton Woods institutions fifty years after their founding, economist David Korten writes, "While these institutions have met their goal, they have failed in their purpose. The world has more poor people today than ever before.... And the planet's ecosystems are deteriorating at an alarming rate." According to Korten, this is due in part to two seriously flawed assumptions: "that economic growth and enhanced world trade would benefit everyone...and that economic growth would not be constrained by the limits of the planet." As evidence of meeting goals, Korten points out that economic growth has increased fivefold, international trade twelve times, and foreign direct investment two to three times the amount of international trade in the fifty years since Bretton Woods.[46]

Our examination of the effects of globalization will focus on people around the globe, with some attention to the environment. In particular, I want to focus on the effects of neoliberalism, which was a definite shift in policy. Economist Mark Weisbrot points out that this is "the heart of the problem: the dominant globalizing

institutions are continuously altering the rules of the game so as to
redistribute income and power upwards."[47]

Susan George asserts that people of the top 20 percent of the
income scale are likely to gain from neoliberalism, and "the higher
you are up the ladder, the more you gain." The bottom 80 percent,
however, "all lose and the lower they are to begin with, the more
they lose proportionately."[48] United Nations Development Program
(UNDP) figures illustrate this point. For example, in 1960 the gap
between the richest 20 percent and the poorest 20 percent of the
world's population was 30 to 1. By 1991 this had grown to 61 to
1, and by 1994 to 74 to 1.

An examination of consumption patterns indicates what this
means in terms of purchasing power. The richest 20 percent worldwide consume 16 times as much—and use 17 times the energy—as
the poorest 20 percent. Altogether, the top one-fifth accounts for 86
percent of all private consumption expenditures. The 1998 UNDP
Human Development Report compared spending on various items
with the additional amount that would be needed—over what is
already spent—to meet the basic needs of all the world's people.
UNDP is not suggesting that if less money were spent on cosmetics
or ice cream, for instance, that the money would go to education
or health care. The purpose of the comparison is to illustrate what
small sums of additional money would be required to meet the basic
needs of all the world's people. In the United States, $8 billion a year
is spent on cosmetics; only $6 billion more than is now spent would
achieve basic education for the entire world. Europeans spend $11
billion on ice cream; only $9 billion more would provide water and
sanitation for all. Europeans and Americans spend $17 billion on
pet food; an additional $13 billion would provide basic health and
nutrition for all. In other words, about $30 billion more than is
now spent would provide basic education, water and sanitation,
and health and nutrition for all. Compare this to the amount spent
globally on advertising or military budgets. Advertising costs over
$430 billion. Military spending topped $719 billion in 1999.[49]

Shalmali Guttal offers insight into this dynamic:

By and large, those who are already wealthy, socially and
politically privileged and have access to capital, higher edu-

cation, productive assets (such as land) and other resources (such as technical know-how and hardware) are usually able to benefit from the economic changes brought about by globalization. But those who are already cash poor, and socially and politically disadvantaged often face tremendous difficulties, and find themselves much worse off than before since they are compelled to operate in a more aggressive competitive economic environment but without the government/public supports that they once relied on.[50]

Free Trade

Supporters of free trade contend that increased economic growth will provide governments more resources to use in environmental clean-up and protection. The data from the developing countries that receive the most new investment—China, Mexico, and Indonesia—is not promising. China has seen nearly a doubling in acid rain, a sharp rise in lung disease, and now has five of the ten world cities with the worst air pollution. Mexico, particularly along the border with the United States, contends with sewage-contaminated water, which spreads gastrointestinal disease—the leading killer of its children. On the U.S. side of the border, hepatitis A rates are three times the national average. Indonesia is second only to Brazil in rainforest depletion. Countries are pressured by the World Bank and the IMF to pay off their outstanding debt through increased export earnings. This means that forests are cut down for timber exports or expansion of agricultural plantations, fishing stocks are depleted, or open-pit mines expanded.[51]

It is instructive to look at what has happened in Great Britain, since it was the first nation to institute neoliberal reforms. According to Susan George, about one person in ten was classed as living below the poverty line before Margaret Thatcher came to power as prime minister in 1979. "Now one person in four, and one child in three is officially poor." This is due, at least in part, to neoliberalism's remuneration of capital to the disadvantage of labor, moving wealth from the bottom of society to the top. Privatization has a similar effect. Before Thatcher's deployment of neoliberalism, "a lot of the public sector in Britain was profitable. Consequently, in 1984, public companies contributed over £7 billion to the treasury. All that money is now going to private shareholders." Noting that privatization is now in effect around the world, George contends, "We should stop talking about privatization and use words that tell the truth: we are talking about alienation and surrender of the product of decades of work by thousands of people to a tiny minority of large investors. This is one of the greatest hold-ups of ours or any generation." Bolivia saw its income from petroleum, which brought in $400 million annually before the industry was privatized, drop to about $80 million in taxes. But what created a mass protest movement was legislation privatizing the water supply, at the recommendation of the World Bank. The law prohibited farmers from building collection tanks for rain water without permission and would have required people to pay the water company for water from wells in their own houses.[52]

The Economic Policy Institute has analyzed the effect of free trade, a key plank in the neoliberal platform, on the United States. They estimate that it may be responsible for at least 20 to 25 percent of the increase in U.S. income inequality since 1979. In 1997, the top 5 percent of households received 21.7 percent of income; the top 20 percent 49.4 percent, the largest share that the top one-fifth has received in any year on record. They assert that between 1979 and 1994, 2.4 million jobs were lost. Of the jobs lost, 83 percent were in manufacturing, which typically provides much better pay than service jobs. There was also phenomenal job growth during this period, but they note that three of every four U.S. jobs in the fastest-growing sectors of employment pay less than a living wage; nearly half of these jobs pay less than half a living wage.[53]

The impact of neoliberalism on Mexico has been devastating. Since 1997 the number of people living in extreme poverty—earning less than $2 a day—has grown by four million. Even with economic growth in 1999, and the creation of more than seven hundred thousand formal-sector jobs, two-thirds of the population—almost two of every three people—remained in poverty. In the two decades between 1960 and 1980, Mexico had reduced its poverty rate from 75 percent to 48 percent. But the trend then reversed.[54]

Mexico's experience is typical of that of other countries in the south. According to Walden Bello, from 1950 to 1980 the rate of economic growth in the south was higher than in the north. During this period, per capita income doubled. The percentage of people living in absolute poverty was reduced, though not their numbers (because of population increase). In contrast, over the last several decades, the numbers of people in absolute poverty have increased. Bello notes that during this period "the pattern of growth in the South was not ideal." Many of these countries had state-owned enterprises and protected industries, which were not particularly efficient. In addition, "environmental destabilization was usually a by-product of industrial growth." He points out, though, that this must be put into context. "Inefficiency did not, for the most part, stifle growth, and state-led or state-assisted capitalism was critical in enhancing national control over the economy." In gauging environmental impact, one can see that it was "puny compared to the national and international ecological consequences of the high-consumption driven, highly wasteful economic strategies pursued by the Northern economies during the same period."[55]

Some scholars and activists charge that this form of globalization is actually a recolonization of the south by the north. An examination of national exports reveals that for some, the colonial division of labor is indeed still in place. "There are thirty-five countries in Latin America, Africa, and Asia that still gain two-fifths or more of export earnings from one or two agricultural or mineral products." For instance, Burundi, Ethiopia, and Uganda in Africa are dependent on coffee exports, with Kenya adding tea to its export of coffee. For Belize and Cuba in Latin America, sugar is still their primary export, while Guyana exports gold along with its sugar. In Asia, Burma still looks to wood and vegetables for export earnings.[56] "Biopiracy" is another example of recolonization. A particularly egregious example is the W. R. Grace Company patenting a biopesticide extracted from the Indian neem tree. This pesticidal extract was long known to and used by Indian people, but the patent process is too expensive for most poor countries to make use of.[57]

The Debt Crisis

Some see the "debt crisis" as yet another form of recolonization. Many of the countries that borrowed money from both private and public institutions during the 1970s and 1980s found it difficult to repay their loans. Some of these countries were dependent on export of commodities whose prices had dropped. The real prices (adjusted for inflation) were 45 percent less in the 1990s than they had been during the 1980s. (Most telling, the prices were 10 percent below their lowest level during the Great Depression.) Thus, their national incomes dropped. At the same time, interest rates skyrocketed—doubling and tripling. In 1980, the debt of poor countries in the south stood at $507 billion; by 1992, it had increased to $1.4 trillion. The interest on this debt ($1.6 trillion) exceeded the outstanding principal (1.4 trillion).[58] Between 1981 and 1997, developing countries—both middle and low-income—paid over $2.9 trillion in principal and interest; yet, the debt of these countries remains at U.S.$2 trillion. "Not since the conquistadors plundered Latin America," said Morris Miller, a former employee of the World Bank, "has the world experienced a [financial] flow in the direction we see today."[59]

Structural adjustment programs (SAPs) were forced on poor countries that needed to reschedule their debt. New loans were often structural adjustment loans (SALs), tied to "reforms" in economic policy rather than funding of particular projects. (This was part of the Washington Consensus discussed above.) SAPs and SALs are based on neoliberalism, and included liberalization of markets, deregulation, privatization, and cuts in social spending.

By 1997, the debt of forty-one highly indebted countries stood at $215 billion, up from $183 billion in 1990. Thirty-three of these forty-one paid $3 in debt service payments to the North for every $1 in development assistance. These countries have been paying a significant share of their total revenues to service their debt. Some pay over half of their government revenues toward debt service, often more than one-fourth of their earnings from exports. Although the majority of the population did not benefit from many of the loans that gave rise to this debt, they are the ones who pay the price. Poor countries are trapped, making never-ending interest payments, which requires them to divert large amounts of resources from health care, education, and food security. For instance, the World Bank discovered that in Zambia, where parents now have to meet 80 percent of education costs because of SAPs, serious drops in school attendance have been observed that disproportionately affect girls. Zambia spends $4 on debt servicing for every dollar spent on health, while infant mortality rates are rising. In Uganda, $3 per person is spent on health care, $17 on repaying its debt; yet, one in every five children dies from a preventable disease before reaching the age of five.[60]

Structural adjustment policies limit the ability of governments of highly indebted poor countries to control their economies and develop policies to meet the needs of their citizens. This is also the case with other aspects of neoliberalism, such as liberalization of trade and capital flows. I have already discussed the charge by former World Bank chief economist Joseph Stiglitz that capital market liberalization was driven by ideology. He was writing in the context of the 1998 Asian financial crisis, which he believes was caused in large part by rigid IMF policies imposed on national governments. Other writers are concerned about the impact of the "casino economy." William Greider observes that government intervention is what has kept recent crises from becoming a worldwide depression, but he points out contradictions in how this intervention has worked. One contradiction is that the costs are socialized; in other words, taxpayers pay for the bailout of banks that have made bad loans or investments. (The cost of bailout during the 1998 Asian crisis was at least $175 billion of public money.) This is in marked contrast to the rhetoric of neoliberalism, which supports limited government intervention and a reduction in social spending. A second contradiction is that some of these private financial institutions are so powerful that they can overwhelm governments. "Managers in national governments are supposedly responsible for overseeing a larger and larger global system of private finance and protecting it from disastrous error. Yet the finance system now has the ability to turn around and punish governments themselves."[61]

Corporate Control

Activist Kevin Danaher also examines the role that corporations play in limiting the ability of governments to control the economy and protect citizens. He asserts that this amounts to the United States and other national governments being "held hostage by the mobility of globalized capital." Corporations "threaten to move out when confronted with higher taxes or stiffer environmental regula-

tions." Provisions of free trade agreements like NAFTA have made
it possible for private investors and corporations to sue governments for profits lost as a result of regulations, "a right they never
had under any previous trade or commercial agreement, such as the
GATT (General Agreement on Tariffs and Trade)." An example of
this is a suit by an American corporation against the Canadian government, which had instituted a ban on the gasoline additive MMT.
Although MMT is effectively banned in the United States, the Ethyl
Corporation suit forced the Canadian Health Ministry to reverse its
ban in July of 1998. The corporation also collected $13 million in
damages for lost profits.[62]

NAFTA has many other harmful impacts. According to Weisbrot,
NAFTA made "it easier and more profitable for U.S. corporations
to relocate to Mexico," which "increases their bargaining power
against workers who try to organize unions. A study commissioned
by the labor secretariat of NAFTA found that the agreement did
in fact have that effect." As Weisbrot claims, these cases support
the charge that globalization is "a means of moving economic
decision-making away from elected bodies such as congresses and
parliaments, and placing more authority in the hands of unelected,
unaccountable institutions such as the IMF, NAFTA, or the transnational corporations themselves." This undermines the institutions
that have alleviated the worst excesses and irrationalities of the
market: the social safety net, environmental legislation, and various forms of financial regulation. Without significant changes, we
can only expect poverty to increase, the gap between the wealthy
and poor to widen, and environmental degradation to intensify.[63]

Held and McGrew conclude, "The particular form taken by economic globalization in the last two decades—neoliberal economic
globalization—has not transcended the old North-South division of
the world but superimposed on it new kinds of division along gender, ethnic, and ecological lines."[64] Activist Shalmali Guttal points
out in her examination of globalization in Asia that export-oriented
economic growth takes place through "commercial harvesting of
natural resources for value added production, increase in plantation and mono-cropping." Privatization, particularly transference
of land, water, and resource rights to private companies, is also a
factor. Both processes, she asserts, gravely threaten biodiversity and

environmental quality. They also alienate local communities—many of which are indigenous—from the resource base that they depend upon and have held in common. Economic globalization has a differential impact on Asian women, due to deep-rooted differences in gender roles and sociocultural expectations. Its impact is at two broad levels. The first is more immediate and experiential, "such as lowered wages, reduced access to land and resources, less food, and greater workload." The second is more structural or strategic, "where impacts are not necessarily visible today, but which lead to a longer-term disempowerment of women." An example is the impact of decreased education of girls on future job opportunities.[65]

Negative impacts like these extend beyond Asia to nearly every corner of the globe. When governments cut social spending, families become more responsible for health, education, and other social services. Since in most societies women traditionally are the caregivers, these responsibilities fall to them. Women are not paid for this work. It increases an already heavy workload (unpaid or low-paid)—subsistence farming, work in the informal sector (selling homegrown fruits and vegetables in local markets, doing piece work at home), or wage labor. Girls may take up part of this load, which takes them out of school. As we saw above, when export processing zones are developed, women usually are the preferred labor force because they are seen as more compliant. This does give women opportunities for work and income, but the wages are low and the working conditions poor. Sociologist Saskia Sassen calls this situation "the feminization of survival." A recently released study of ten African countries, *Demanding Dignity: Women Confronting Economic Reforms in Africa*, notes that although African women could benefit from economic restructuring, "all too often policy decisions reinforce or aggravate existing inequalities... in many cases, economic restructuring has increased poverty and further marginalized women." The study raises questions about gender and social justice in several areas, including structural adjustment programs, export processing zones, loan and financial services, and monetary policy related to agriculture and food security.[66]

Writing on the effect on women, Patricia Connelly concludes, "Restructuring and structural adjustment in the political economies of both the South and North increases the workload of most women,

perpetuates the traditional gender division of labor, reinforces un-
equal gender relations, and maintains the notion that women are
naturally suited for caregiving work."[67] In a review of the literature
and detailed empirical analysis, Nancy Forsythe, Roberto Patricio
Korzeniewicz, and Valerie Durrant conclude that women's status
overall tends to advance with economic development, but that inequality between women and men is less impervious to change. In
fact, economic growth can increase gender inequality.[68]

Increasing Migration

Another impact of economic globalization is increasing migration.
Neoliberalism advocates the free flow of trade and capital, but not
of people. It does, though, create conditions that encourage migration. "The single most important effect of foreign investment
in export production is the uprooting of people from traditional
modes of existence . . . transforming people into migrant workers
and, potentially, into emigrants." About 2 percent of the global
population—one hundred million people—are immigrants. Most
of these are workers following economic opportunities, in part because opportunities at home have dwindled. Many send economic
resources home; these are called remittances. The amount that immigrants living in the United States sent home more than doubled
between 1985 and 1996, from $9.2 to $20.7 billion. In 1998, the
total global estimate for remittances was more than $70 billion.[69]

To appreciate the significance of this amount, Sassen points out,
we must relate it to the GDP and foreign currency reserves of each
country involved. In fact, some countries have made "export" of
their citizens as laborers part of their economic development program. The Philippines is a major sender of migrants generally and
of women particularly—twelve women for each man. "Remittances
were the third largest source of foreign exchange over the last several years." Bangladesh has many of its working population in the
Middle East, Japan, and several European countries; "their remittances represent about a third of foreign exchange."[70] Most of these
workers are exploited and many are sexually harassed and abused.

Economic globalization, particularly in its neoliberal form, has
also led to an increase in "illegal" immigration. NAFTA made provisions for businesspeople to operate in a country other than where

they hold citizenship—a "privatization of immigration." No such provisions were made for low-wage workers. I recently saw first-hand some of the effects of this. As part of the Borderlinks program, mentioned in the preface, we talked to people in the border town of Douglas, Arizona, to learn more about immigration. Douglas is now the busiest illegal border crossing area on the thousand-mile-long U.S.-Mexican border, since the U.S. effort to crack down on illegal immigration in the 1980s and 1990s. (This included a doubling of both the funding for border patrol and related programs and the number of agents between 1993 and 1997.) As it became more difficult to cross over along the California and Texas sections of the border, border crossers without documents shifted to Arizona. Operation Enhanced Safeguard in Douglas brought a dramatic increase in agents—five hundred in a station built for eighty. There are fifteen hundred agents along the Arizona section of the border, who sometimes "round up" eight hundred to one thousand people per day. Most are from Mexico, 15 to 20 percent from Central America, some from Europe or Asia.[71]

While we were at the U.S. Border Patrol station, we saw a bus arrive carrying seventy-nine young people, including two pregnant women. All had been caught in just a few hours that morning. When new "detainees" are brought in, they are taken into holding tanks and their identities established though a sophisticated "Identi-kit," They are then taken back to other side of the border, unless they are held to be charged, which is done to "coyotes," who are in charge of the crossing, or to people who have been caught over five times. We did not have time to see the weapons area, but were told they are state of the art. We did see the intelligence center, with sixteen separate screens showing what video cameras spread along the border have picked up. One of the station leaders stressed to us that they are "just enforcing the law and protecting the U.S." He admitted, though, that if he had to face the conditions that some of the border crossers faced, he might do the same thing. We also met with Father Bob, a priest at a Douglas area church. He told of finding baby shoes, family pictures, even corpses in the desert where people try to cross. In just six weeks between August 1, 2000, and our visit in mid-September, eight died in the Douglas area alone. Since 1995, over six hundred people have died attempting to cross the U.S.-Mexican border.

Susan George asserts, "Neo-liberalism has changed the fundamental nature of politics." In the past, politics was mainly about "who ruled whom and who got what share of the pie." George knows that parts of these significant questions remain. She contends, though, that "the great new central question of politics is... *'Who has a right to live and who does not.'* " She concludes that "radical exclusion is now the order of the day."[72] In this chapter, we have seen that more and more of the world has been drawn into the realm of capitalist globalization. This is a process of inclusion in profit-generating dynamics; yet, the majority of people are excluded from its benefits. The next chapter focuses more closely on production chains for food and clothing to uncover the harsh realities behind the food we eat and the clothes we wear.

Questions for Discussion

1. What changes has the expansion of global trade and investment made in your life, your family, your community?

2. Do you know people who have benefited from globalization? Suffered from it? Have you visited countries other than your own? How different were living conditions there?

3. Discuss the impact of globalization on women. Do you agree that generally they are more burdened than men? What changes could be made to lessen this impact?

4. Do you agree that concentrated economic power threatens democracy? What are your reasons for your view?

5. Do the rules of the global economy seem unfair to you? How would you change them?

Additional Resources

Anderson, Sarah, and John Cavanagh, with Thea Lee and the Institute for Policy Studies. *Field Guide to the Global Economy.* New York: New Press, 2000. A very readable guide, with lots of tables, graphs, and even some cartoons.

Daly, Herman, and John Cobb. *For the Common Good: Redirecting the Economy toward Community, the Environment, and a Sustainable Future.* Updated and expanded. Boston: Beacon Press, 1994.

van Drimmelen, Rob. *Faith in a Global Economy: A Primer for Christians.* Geneva: World Council of Churches, 1998. An interesting and accessible text.

Finn, Daniel. *Just Trading: On the Ethics and Economics of International Trade.* Nashville: Abingdon Press, 1996. A thoughtful analysis by a scholar who is both an ethicist and an economist.

Hardisty, Jean. "Libertarianism and Civil Society: The Romance of Free Market Capitalism." *The Public Eye* 12, no. 1 (spring 1998): 1–18. A useful overview of libertarianism in the United States.

Held, David, and Anthony McGrew, eds. *The Global Transformations Reader: An Introduction to the Globalization Debate.* Cambridge: Polity Press, 2000. Pp. 100–102. An excellent scholarly introduction to globalization.

Heilbroner, Robert, and Lester Thurow. *Economics Explained.* Revised and updated. New York: Simon and Schuster, 1994. Pp. 130–46, 261–70. A useful discussion of how money is created.

Hinga, Teresia. "The Gikuyu Theology of Land and Environmental Justice." Pp. 172–84 in *Women Healing Earth: Third World Women on Ecology, Feminism, and Religion,* ed. Rosemary Radford Ruether. Maryknoll, N.Y.: Orbis Books, 1996. An insightful analysis of the impact of colonialism on women and land in Kenya.

Johnston, Carol. *The Wealth or Health of Nations: Transforming Capitalism from Within.* Cleveland: Pilgrim Press, 1998. An excellent critical discussion of economic theory, beginning with Adam Smith.

Martinez, Elizabeth, and Arnoldo García. "What Is 'Neo-Liberalism'? A Brief Definition." www.globalexchange.org. A readable online account of neoliberalism.

Multinational Monitor. www.essential.org/monitor. An excellent monthly publication that tracks activities and abuses of TNCs.

Owensby, Walter L. *Economics for Prophets: A Primer on Concepts, Realities, and Values in Our Economic System.* Grand Rapids: Eerdmans, 1988.

Rasmussen, Larry. *Earth Community, Earth Ethics.* Maryknoll, N.Y.: Orbis Books, 1996. A groundbreaking ethical analysis of the ecological crisis.

Willett, Susan. "Globalisation and Insecurity in the Twenty-First Century." Geneva: United Nations Institute for Disarmament Research, October 2000. www.unog.ch/unidir. A draft discussion paper circulated for comment, this is a suggestive treatment of the connections between globalization, civil conflict, and the arms trade.

World Survey on the Role of Women in Development: Globalization, Gender and Work. New York: United Nations, 1999. An invaluable compendium of data and analysis.

TWO

What Does Globalization Have to Do with Daily Life?

All people are interdependent.... We are everlasting debtors to known and unknown men and women.... At the table we drink coffee which is provided for us by a South American, or tea by a Chinese or cocoa by a west African. Before we leave for our jobs we are already beholden to more than half the world.
— MARTIN LUTHER KING JR., *Where Do We Go from Here: Chaos or Community?*, 1967

Behind the perfect-looking tomato, there are thousands of hidden oppressive realities.... How can we raise our consciousness so that we are aware of the food we are eating, where it comes from and who, in fact, puts it on our tables?
— EGLA MARTINEZ-SALAZAR, "The Poisoning of Indigenous Migrant Women Workers and Children: From Deadly Colonialism to Toxic Globalization," 1999

I made elegant Reebok, Puma, and Nike shoes for eleven years. But look at what I wear on my feet—a cheap pair of plastic sandals. I am like those who build but are homeless and those who till the soil but are hungry.
— LAURA, a sacked Filipina factory worker, 1996

Many celebrate the global trade, if not interdependence, that brings an amazing variety of foods to our tables. Not so many look behind the products to ask about production and distribution systems. At what human cost are imports produced? When polled, most Americans report that they do not want to buy goods produced by exploited labor. But how can we know? And what can we do about it?

Where were the clothes you are wearing produced? The tags can be misleading. "Made in the USA" might mean Saipan, a U.S.

44

territory where young women are recruited from China and other countries—at great cost to their family for their transportation and guestworker papers—to work at wages below the U.S. minimum in sweatshop conditions. What about the tomatoes you bought at your local market? Certainly they aren't produced under exploitative conditions, are they? Likely they were—planted, tended, and picked by low-paid migrant workers who are exposed to deadly pesticides. When we think about these conditions, we ask, "Globalization at what price?"

In chapter 1, I examined the dynamics of globalization and its impact on people and the environment around the world. This chapter explores these forces in more depth in the United States and globally, with food and clothing as case studies. The focus is processes of production and distribution of food and clothing, with particular attention to North America after NAFTA. I want to show that these forces are not natural, but "man-made rules of the game" that can be challenged (the topic of chapters 4 and 5).

Food: Enough for All?

The World Bank reports that although "human conditions have improved more in the past century than in the rest of history," as many as half of the children under the age of five in poorer countries suffer from eating too little food as compared to fewer than 5 percent of children in well-off countries. Five times as many children die in poorer countries before reaching age five (five per hundred) than in high-income countries (less than one per hundred). Since "global wealth, global connections, and technological capabilities have never been greater," why do so many children suffer from malnutrition?[1]

Causes of Hunger

Before we examine food production and distribution more carefully, we must first address some myths about hunger. Two especially common myths are that there are too many people and that there is not enough food. Like hunger, rapid population growth "results from underlying inequities that deprive people, especially poor women, of economic opportunity and security," the Institute for

Food and Development Policy (IFDP) argues.[2] A study by another group, the International Food Policy Research Institute (IFPRI), supports this claim. They examined factors that helped reduce child malnutrition by 15 percent in the developing world between 1970 and 1995, and found that "women's education and status within the household contribute more than 50 percent to the reduction of child malnutrition." These same factors contribute to a reduction in the rate of population growth.[3]

Nor is widespread hunger caused by a lack of food. The IFDP shows that "the problem is that *many people are too poor to buy readily available food*." Even countries with many hungry people have enough food for their people; in fact, they export more food and agricultural products than they import. A farmer in Zaire, referring to a scheme to switch land used for food into export-crop production, observed, "If you have to buy food, you will never have enough." The IFDP contends that neither the free market nor free trade will end hunger. As they point out, market efficiencies "can only work to eliminate hunger...when purchasing power is widely dispersed." We have seen that nearly two billion people live on $2 or less a day; their purchasing power is very small.[4]

Sociologist and food activist Harriet Friedman notes that more of the world's people, especially those from peasant communities, "work to produce food that they may not ever eat themselves. Instead, they are supplying world markets and often eat what comes back to them from world markets."[5] However, they need cash income to purchase this food.

Mexico is a good example of this trend. Not long ago, Mexico was nearly self-sufficient in its production of basic foodstuffs like corn, beans, and rice. As recently as 1989, Mexico imported virtually no rice. It now imports over half of the rice it consumes, becoming the second-largest market for U.S. rice. Just before NAFTA took effect, Mexico imported only 2 percent of its corn. Now, about one-fourth of the corn consumed in Mexico is imported from the United States.[6]

Imports hurt Mexican farmers. The National Association of Commercial Corporations reported in January 2000 that bean producers in five Mexican states grew enough beans (1.2 million metric tons) last year to meet the needs of Mexican consumers. However, a huge domestic surplus was created by the one hundred thousand metric tons of duty-free beans from the United States and Argentina, which depressed prices for beans. But increased supplies have not generally led to lower consumer prices. Their figures show a 10 percent decline in domestic consumption of corn and beans in 1999, primarily because of high prices. (Remember my grocery visit in the preface?) For instance, the price of tortillas went up 350 percent in four years, due in part to the Mexican government's 1999 decision to eliminate all tortilla price controls and subsidies. However, minimum-wage workers will receive only a 10 percent raise.[7]

How are people in the United States implicated in this? One can see that free markets and free trade, as advocated by the neoliberal global economic model, do not seem to be a solution to hunger. But very few Americans are engaged in farming anymore. Indeed, that is the case. However, if we think about where the food we eat comes from and how it gets to our tables, we will find those "thousands of hidden oppressive realities." Deborah Barndt did this by building on a "commodity chain analysis" to trace "the tomato chain" from Mexico to Canada, what she calls the "NAFTA food chain." She examined three "interlocking processes": (1) raw material production, (2) combined processing, packaging, and exporting activities, and (3) marketing and consumptive activities.[8]

Barndt begins at the end of the chain, which is where consumers come into the picture. She examines workers' experiences at McDonald's restaurants, where many tomatoes are consumed in one form or another, and at a supermarket chain, where tomatoes would be purchased for home use. She then moves one step back in the chain to a Del Monte food-processing plant in Mexico, where ketchup is produced; and then finally to the source, an agribusiness in central Mexico that grows and packs tomatoes. She discovers two interrelated processes: "McDonaldization," which began in the north and is spreading to the south, and "maquilization," which began in the south and is now appearing in the north.

"McDonaldization," as described by George Ritzer, "is the model that the fast-food restaurant has offered as a way to reorganize work in all other sectors," including supermarkets. The use of flexible part-time labor is central to this model. Other important norms include "efficiency, predictability, calculability or quantifiability, substitution of non-human technology, and control."[9] Flexible labor is usually female labor, based on cultural assumptions about women and work. When this model is adopted by other sectors, such as supermarkets, it means lower wages, fewer hours, and loss of benefits—especially for women, who comprise the majority of service workers.

The Maquilization of Agriculture

"Maquilization," which began in the free trade zones of Mexico, now refers to "a more generalized work process characterized by (1) the feminization of the labour force, (2) extreme segmentation of skill categories, (3) the lowering of real wages and (4) a non-union orientation," according to Barndt. Full-time, but not necessarily stable, employment is available in the "traditional maquila sectors, such as the garment and electronic industries" (which I will examine in the next part of this chapter). NAFTA made it possible for maquilas to develop throughout Mexico. And what Barndt describes as "agromaquilas" depend on part-time, temporary, mainly female labor. For instance, the Del Monte food-processing plant adds part-time, female workers during the peak season. "These women sometimes sit in the waiting room of the plant, hoping for a few hours of work, which are determined day by day." The agromaquila that grows and packages tomatoes "employs mestizos from the local area for the jobs of cultivating the tomato plants, while hundreds of poor Indigenous workers, brought in by trucks and housed in conditions of squalor in makeshift camps, do much of the picking during the three-to-five month harvest season."[10]

Egla Martinez-Salazar, quoted at the beginning of this chapter, migrated with her family as a mestiza child to work on coffee and cotton plantations in Guatemala. One of her sisters died "because of exposure to pesticides and lack of proper food, medical care and adequate housing while working on the plantation." During her research in Mexico, she found similar conditions. Most tomato pickers and packers are not given adequate information about the dangers of pesticides. She concludes that such information is "practically hidden." Instructions about toxicity and precautions are in English. The special gloves and masks recommended by the pesticide manufacturers are usually not provided for the workers by plantation managers.[11]

Migrant workers in the United States and Canada also suffer from these conditions. Antoineta Barron interviewed women migrant workers in both Mexico and Canada, where they come under a guestworker program. Although women working in Mexican fields clearly get "the worse deal" (both their working and living conditions have deteriorated due to an overabundance of workers), there were some similarities in their experiences. Neither group is paid for overtime. Although they may receive medical attention if they are ill or injured, they are not paid for time taken from the workday for medical visits or recuperation.[12] It is appropriate to call this work "sweatshops in the fields."

Many of the farmworkers in the United States are undocumented immigrants. Martinez-Salazar observes that indigenous communities have been adversely affected by government industrialization and agricultural modernization policies. Communities cope "by sending young men and women into forced migration to urban cities, within Mexico or to the United States, to find work."[13] Harriet Friedman sees population growth as a factor in migration. She argues that over time, peasants could no longer provision themselves from the land they received after the Mexican revolution. First men, and then women, left the *ejido* (communal lands) to find work in cities, in export processing zones—maquiladoras—on the U.S. border, or in the U.S."[14] This situation has been exacerbated by the breakup of communal land holdings under NAFTA.

The county I live in, which abuts Los Angeles County, is a large agricultural producer, mainly of fruits and vegetables. A major freeway runs through some prime agricultural land, and from it one can often see scores of farmworkers stooped over, planting, weeding, picking the food that will be on our tables. Wages are low, conditions poor, but families pull together to survive. Many families have been here for decades, and some have moved into better-paid, more secure employment. Some children from these families come to the university where I teach. This past year, three young Latinas from farmworker families took my environmental ethics course. They became very interested in the issue of pesticides, in part because of a chapter by Cesar Chavez on this topic in our text. Although one young woman's sister had been ill because of pesticide exposure, they reported that they were not aware of how widespread or serious the problem is.

Conditions in California's Central Valley are worse. The top three farm counties there produce $7 billion of California's roughly $26 billion in annual crop sales. But they are also home to seven of the state's ten poorest unincorporated communities. There is a surplus of workers; according to the U.S. Department of Labor, "An estimated 700,000 farmworkers chase about 400,000 jobs in California." Many growers use contractors, who take responsibility for hiring, paying, housing, and transporting the workers. During harvest season, some contractors use two-bedroom houses, where they put as many as twenty-five workers. They get a kickback from the owner for every worker who sleeps there.

Three hundred miles south in the Imperial Valley, "some farmworkers—who earn, at best, the minimum wage of $5.75 an hour—paid $5 a night to sleep in an overcrowded trailer. Others made their homes in the shade of cars in public parking lots. They used two filthy outhouses and bathed in a nearby ditch, in runoff from the fields." Workers wages have fallen while farm profits have hit record highs. Benefits won during the farmworker movement thirty years ago have been lost. The use of contractors has contributed to this deterioration. These are just some of the hidden oppressive realities in the production system that brings food to our tables.[15]

Poultry production would be another good example of hidden oppressive realities. We could begin with the subcontracting of production to factory farms by huge agribusinesses, which shifts the risks from themselves to rural families, in places like Tennessee, struggling to survive after their jobs have fled to places with even cheaper labor. We could then move on to the processing plants, increasingly staffed by Mexican and Central American immigrants at low wages in deteriorating working conditions. We could remember the twenty-five workers, primarily women and disproportionately African American, who died in the 1991 chicken-processing plant fire in North Carolina. Fifty-six of the two hundred workers were seriously injured.[16] There are similar realities in the production system that puts clothes on our bodies.

Apparel: At What Cost?

Over half of the clothing sold in the United States is made in factories in Asia, Central and Latin America, and the Caribbean, usually in maquiladoras or export processing zones by U.S. companies. The great majority of workers are women, particularly young women. In the 1960s, most clothing sold in the United States was made by American workers earning a living wage, under conditions closely monitored by labor unions and federal inspectors. Fifty years of reforms, dating to the 1911 Triangle Shirtwaist Factory fire that killed 146 workers, mostly young women, began to erode in the 1970s. In the 1980s, the number of federal labor inspectors was cut from sixteen hundred to about seven hundred. Today there are about eight hundred inspectors to police workplaces employing more than one million garment workers. Lured by lower labor costs and the desire to increase profit margins, manufacturers and retailers began to move production overseas in the 1970s. Domestic shops moved away from union labor and began to rely on nonunion workers and undocumented immigrants.[17]

Sweatshops in the United States

On August 2, 1995, seventy-two Thai nationals—nearly all young women—were discovered in virtual slavery in El Monte, in Los Angeles County, California, an area about an hour from where I live and work. These garment workers, who had been recruited under false pretenses and brought illegally to the United States, were sewing clothing for seventeen hours a day for about sixty-nine cents an hour. They had been forced for over two years to work and live in a barbed-wire compound, their passports taken from them when they were smuggled into the United States. The clothes they made were sold at stores where many of us shop—Target, Mervyn's, Sears, even upscale Nordstrom's.[18]

　　Although this incident of abuse and virtual enslavement of workers in El Monte is outrageous, to focus on it is to miss the point. "Their plight is not some aberrant phenomenon, a freak occurrence in freakish Los Angeles," Christopher Scheer writes. "It is simply the outer limit in a rainbow of exploitation—of women, of poor people, of garment workers."[19] For half of all U.S. apparel factories are "sweatshops that routinely deny minimum wage or overtime to workers," according to the U.S. Department of Labor. The U.S. General Accounting Office defines a sweatshop as "an employer that violates more than one federal or state labor law governing minimum wage and overtime, child labor, industrial homework, occupational safety and health, workers compensation, or industry regulation."

There are more than 4,500 sweatshops in New York City alone, employing some 50,000 workers. Southern California has more than 6,500 manufacturers and sewing contractors, employing more than 140,000 workers—85 percent of whom are women, mostly women of color—documented and undocumented immigrants from Mexico, Central America, and Asia. People are pushed out of their rural homelands by factors such as the inability to survive by subsistence farming, change in governmental policies, and desire for more opportunity, and are pulled by job possibilities in the United States.[20]

A recent U.S. Department of Labor survey (August 2000) in southern California reports, "Only one-third of the garment factories inspected complied with federal minimum wage and overtime laws—meaning that 67 percent of the region's factories can be classified as sweatshops.... In total, $900,000 in back wages was found to be owed to 1,400 workers." The actual number is probably higher, as only registered shops were investigated. In a separate survey of the region, the California Department of Occupational Safety and Health found that "98 percent of garment factories were in violation of health and safety laws and that 47 percent were violations serious enough to cause severe injury or death. Violations include exposed electrical equipment, blocked exits and unguarded machines."[21]

In addition to the desire of manufacturers and retailers to gain record profits by cutting labor costs, U.S. immigration policy and anti-immigrant sentiment are significant dimensions of the existence of sweatshops. "Employer sanctions, guestworker programs, and various reform acts have proven to be detrimental towards garment workers' rights by giving employers the power to lower wages, extend work hours, disregard health and safety regulations, and suppress unionizing efforts." Anti-immigrant sentiment creates fear among immigrants about asserting their rights. Employers are aware of the limited resources that immigrants have in asserting their rights. Among the tactics they use against workers are: "convincing documented workers to accept lower wages and overtime work by warning them that they can easily be replaced by undocumented workers; retaliating against organizing efforts by firing workers; reporting the undocumented to the INS; and moving factories underground or closing down shops to force employees out of work."[22] The mother of a student at my university, a documented immigrant from Guatemala, testified during a campus forum on sweatshops to these conditions. She had worked for over a decade for a contractor who unreasonably limited bathroom breaks; she had never had a paid vacation. She was afraid to complain because she needed her job to help support her family and put her children through school.

Human Rights Watch recently issued a report documenting that "freedom of association is a right under severe, often buckling pressure when workers in the United States try to exercise it." U.S. labor law and its enforcement do not measure up to international human rights standards. The report includes sections on immigrant workers, which support the charges made by Sweatshop Watch.[23]

Mexico

Some companies, like Guess?, have closed shop in southern California and moved their production to Mexico. In their analysis of this industry, sociologists Edna Bonacich and Richard Appelbaum conclude, "Smaller companies and those that specialize in fashion, for which short runs and styles constantly are changing, will remain. These companies need a quick turnaround, and they need the smaller factories characteristic of the industry in LA." But for the production of basics, like T-shirts, which involve big runs of the same line and styles that do not constantly change, companies are likely to leave Los Angeles. In fact, they found that Mexico has passed Hong Kong and is close to China in terms of the dollar value of combined textile and apparel exports to the U.S., since the passage and implementation of NAFTA in 1994.[24]

The U.S.-Mexican border may be the only place in the world where a first world and a third world country meet. In her work on this border, Gloria Anzaldúa vividly describes it as *"una herida abierta* [an open wound] where the Third World grates against the first and bleeds."[25] Although Bonacich and Appelbaum's work focused on Los Angeles, their book does report on conditions in Tehuacán, Mexico, where the Guess? company moved its production. Tehuacán is fast becoming a center of denim production for manufacturers in Los Angeles and elsewhere. Tehuacán, a fast-growing city of over three hundred thousand, is a few hours' drive southeast of Mexico City. "It is the second-largest city in Puebla, an impoverished region populated mainly by indigenous peoples who provide a large and hungry source of labor." There are an estimated four hundred sewing factories, which "reportedly sew and stone wash jeans for such major labels as Polo, Lee, Bugle Boy, Cherokee, and Levi's, and for Guess, since it decided to move out of LA." Appelbaum was part of a delegation of human rights observers in February 1998 who "heard evidence from local workers of many forms of exploitation and mistreatment in the factories, and of a pervasive atmosphere of fear." Wages at that time ranged from $25 to $50 (U.S. dollars) for a workweek of forty-eight to sixty hours; forced (and unpaid) overtime was often required to meet production quotas. The observers were told that "minors as young as thirteen... were reported to be working alongside adults under unsafe conditions that sometimes resulted in accidents." The factories were "enormous and prosperous-looking"—also frequently windowless—"surrounded by high walls and locked gates." These were a "stark contrast to the sprawling colonias, where workers lived in make-shift, dirt-floor shacks, typically without access to running water, electricity, sewage, schools, or other basic urban amenities." The final report of the delegation concluded, "What the delegation found in Tehuacán, Mexico, is that worker rights are not respected and codes of conduct are not enforced; instead they are subordinated to the global search for cheap labor. Humane treatment of maquiladora workers and respect for their rights are traded off for the mass production of on-time and high-quality clothing."[26]

As I explained in the preceding chapter, Mexico started the Border Industrialization Program (maquiladora) in 1965 to provide employment for Mexican seasonal migrant laborers, mainly male, who needed a way to make a living after the United States ended the Bracero Program, which permitted them to work in the United States. As Altha Cravey notes, the maquiladora program dramatically changed the local economy in most border cities, from Matamoras to Tijuana.[27] I want to tell about Agua Prieta and Nogales, both on the Arizona border. On a recent visit to the area as part of a Borderlinks experiential education program, I talked with people there.

Maquilas were first built in Agua Prieta and Nogales in 1966, but it was not until the early 1980s that they took off. A factor in this was currency devaluation: in 1980 the exchange rate was 12 pesos to $1; by 1990 it was 3,000 pesos to $1 (it was then changed so that 3,000 pesos became 3 pesos; the exchange rate in the fall of 2000 was about 10 to 1). Labor became much cheaper. "The number of maquilas increased to 3,384 in 1999, up from 620 in 1980. The plants employ 1.1 million workers, mostly women, near the U.S. border."[28] Agua Prieta has forty-two maquilas, which employ about eighteen thousand workers; Nogales has around one hundred maquilas. Many different products are assembled here, including electronics, which as I indicated in the preface may be used by the U.S. military or by consumers in their televisions or stereos. Some clothing is also made here.

Our Borderlinks group met with workers affiliated with base communities at a Roman Catholic parish in Agua Prieta. As we entered the sanctuary, which was stark by Roman Catholic standards, I was struck by the altar. The focus was sculptures of the Holy Family—working! Mary was spinning, Joseph sawing, and the child Jesus hammering. We were warmly welcomed and ate dinner with some base community pastoral workers—wonderful, wise women—and members of some workers' groups they'd formed, mainly women and their children. After the meal we listened to their stories.

Pola told us that it was through their study of scripture, what she called a liberating gospel—using the method of see, think, and act—that they felt called to reach out and work with poor and exploited members of their community. Pola and the other pastoral workers made rounds—pastoral visits—through the parish after working hours to meet workers and listen to their concerns. Eventually, some would join together in groups to share their problems. A Border

Workers Committee from the church teaches workers their rights. The Committee for Justice in the Maquiladoras, a useful resource for this work, provides themes and workshops on problems like toxics in the work environment. The workers report some small successes, such as getting legal severance pay—which companies often don't pay—when their employer, an electronics firm, left for Asia.

We learned that most workers make $50 to $55 a week for six ten-hour days. A study they did found that a very moderate cost of living requires 1,800 pesos a week—about $200 a week—for a family of four. Workers survive through a variety of strategies, including pooling income, or living in substandard housing with minimal utilities. For example, although my host's house had lights and plumbing, only the sink and toilet in the bathroom were connected to the water lines. Water for use in the kitchen and shower had to be carried in and heated on the gas stove. She connected the electric wires to her car battery at night to light the house. After visiting a colonia, I realized that these conditions were relatively luxurious.

The colonia we visited was in Nogales, where much of the housing in the city has been developed in this way. When people come in from rural areas to work in the maquilas, they often find a shortage of affordable housing. Colonias develop in part because the Mexican Constitution permits people to squat on land that has not been used for a period of ten years or more. This usually takes the form of a "land invasion," often organized by women. After living there for five years, the people can apply to legally buy the land from the owner. Then they struggle for amenities—electricity, running water, sewers, roads—which can take another five years. Though life in the colonias is hard, it is one way that poor people can make a home in the urban areas where the jobs are.

We visited a colonia called Colosio, which does not have utilities yet. As we walked through the dusty roads, I saw flowers planted—zinnias in a tire beside the road, rose bushes outside some of the homes made from scrap wood and tin, and in some cases, cardboard. Water is brought in by tank trunks and costs the people dearly, given their low wages. Car batteries are stacked in the houses to provide some energy, for instance, to occasionally watch a very small television. Since there is no plumbing, people build outhouses. We had lunch with the residents, many of whom work in the maquilas. Our hosts welcomed us graciously and shared their stories of their struggle to survive. A young woman in the home I visited is finishing her schooling in a secretarial program. She will soon get her certificate, but told us that secretarial jobs are not easy to find in Nogales. She hopes to find one.

We also talked with workers from a T-shirt factory in Agua Prieta. They have been on strike since September of 1999 to keep the owner from moving the factory to Thailand without giving them their severance pay. With the help of the Border Workers Committee from the church, they consulted a lawyer. Their case went to court, where the judge ruled in their favor. He gave them the remaining equipment in the factory to sell. While they are waiting for a good buyer, they guard the factory day and night to keep the equipment from being removed. Those who have found other jobs give part of their pay to support those who guard the factory at night. The church and the Maquila Organizing Project in Tucson support four day guards. Esther, coordinator of the base community, told us that they try to act as early Christians did—when things were held in common, and members of the community shared with each other.

Asia

What are conditions like in Thailand, to where both the electronics and the apparel factories from Agua Prieta fled? As we have seen, capital searches the globe for cheap labor and lax safety and environmental laws. So as we might expect, conditions in Thailand are even worse. In fact, the worst industrial fire in the history of capitalism occurred at a toy factory on the outskirts of Bangkok, at the Kader Industrial Toy Company, on May 10, 1993. Kader employed three thousand workers who made plastic dolls and stuffed toys to be sold in the United States. The company was located in a thriving industrial zone for garment, toys, and electronics firms, which employed more than fifty thousand people, most of them from the Thai countryside. The official count of the victims of the fire was 188 dead and 469 injured, but the actual toll was much higher. The four-story factory buildings collapsed quickly, and many bodies were incinerated. The structures had been built cheaply, without concrete reinforcements. Although Thai law required that fire-escape stairways in large factories be 16 to 33 feet in width, Kader's were only 4½ feet. Main doors were locked, and many windows barred.

All but fourteen of the dead were women, most of them young—some as young as thirteen. Six months later, eighty-four women died and dozens of others were severely burned at a toy factory fire in China. There have been many other fires with fewer victims. In contrast to the uproar following the Triangle Shirtwaist fire, there was no political or consumer response. According to William Greider, the story was on page 25 of the *Washington Post,* and was a brief item on page 6 of the *Financial Times,* which claims to be the daily newspaper of the global economy.[29]

Workers at Kader earned about 100 bahts a day (U.S.$4), the official minimum—not a living wage. But many at the factory—new entrants—earned only $2 to $3 a day, during a required probationary period. Only one hundred of the three thousand workers were legally designated employees; the rest were "contract workers" without permanent rights and benefits—a system used more and more in the United States. When Thailand raised its minimum wage, many firms moved to China, Indonesia, and Vietnam, where wages are even lower.

The development of computer and telecommunications technology has facilitated this global spread of production. It makes it possible for corporations to track and control production that they can contract out anywhere. Wal-Mart developed the leading retail strategy, what some call the "Wal-Mart model." This is a "super-efficient production process in which each operation—buying products from manufacturers, distributing them to retail stores, and selling them to customers—is linked to the next in a continuous 'just-in-time' chain."[30] This model has made Wal-Mart the world's largest retailer; its economy is as large as that of 160 countries combined. Wal-Mart claims to have a "buy American" policy, but the great majority of the apparel it sells is produced in other countries. It uses over one thousand sweatshops in China alone.

A recent National Labor Committee (NLC) report describes conditions in a handbag factory in China that makes Kathie Lee handbags sold at Wal-Mart. The average take-home pay is the equivalent of three U.S. cents an hour, or $3.10 for a ninety-eight-hour workweek. The highest wage found was only ten cents an hour. (Shifts are fourteen hours, seven days a week, every week.) Workers are housed sixteen to a room, fed two poor meals a day, and subject to physical and verbal abuse. The workers are charged for dorm and living expenses. Because of these charges, almost half the workers actually owed the company money at the end of the month. The NLC charges that the workers are held as indentured servants, by having their identification documents confiscated by factory management; workers are allowed to leave the factory for only ninety minutes a day. Eight hundred of the thousand workers in the plant were fired for fighting for their rights.[31] *Business Week* magazine verified these conditions and described what it called "the disaster" of Wal-Mart's self-monitoring system, which failed to uncover this situation.[32]

Unjust Systems

As with food production, workers at both ends of the system of production and distribution experience unjust conditions. Workers in Wal-Mart stores in the United States are paid minimum wage; even department heads begin at just $8 an hour. It is difficult to get real full-time work at Wal-Mart, because the company defines "full-time" as twenty-eight hours a week. Workers must contribute 40 percent of the costs of health benefits, which are available to full-timers. Employee stock ownership takes the place of a pension plan, but high turnover and low pay means that less than 2 percent of workers have accumulated fifty thousand dollars or more. Furthermore, many of these workers depend on this work for their long-term livelihood. There is little opportunity for advancement because the job hierarchy is extremely flat.[33] Since some Wal-Mart stores now have a McDonald's restaurant located in them, we have come full circle. We are back to McDonald's, the starting point in our examination of the "hidden oppressive realities" in the systems of production and distribution of food and clothing.

As we have seen, these systems are intersections of unjust gender, racial/ethnic, and class systems within and between nations. The work of three different scholars offers insight into these intersections. Pierre Bordieu believes that the casualization of work I have described is part of a new mode of domination "based on the creation of a generalized and permanent state of insecurity aimed at forcing workers into submission, into the acceptance of exploitation." This process is facilitated by the competition that is set up between workers in more and less socially advanced countries when production moves from one space to another.[34]

In her study of women and work in Mexican maquiladoras, Altha Cravey identified both factory and gender regimes that link production and social reproduction. The import substitution industrialization regime, developed after the Mexican revolution, provided well-paid jobs with good benefits for men and encouraged housewife roles for women. The state, along with labor unions, was the primary source of social provision—health care, childcare, and housing. The maquila regime, which began in the 1960s and is becoming the dominant model, provides low-paid jobs—primarily for women—with few benefits. The state is withdrawing from social provisioning, which is being left to individual workers and maquila owners. This has brought a change in the gender regime. Fewer women are full-time housewives; some men share household chores, particularly childcare.[35]

Patricia Fernandez-Kelly approaches this reality through the concepts of gender and class. She suggests, "Gender is better understood as the pivot around which class divisions organize. Female subordination can be properly explained only as part of larger orders of domination that critically affect men." Kelly believes that "women's dependent status acts as a two-edged sword," particularly if it is backed by law and custom. On the one hand, it facilitates the maintenance "of an exploitable labor pool within the domestic realm." On the other hand, women's dependent status also functions to control men, especially men of the working classes. "Until recently, equating masculinity with the ability to support women and children functioned as a potent mechanism to secure male compliance." This was true, according to Kelly, "not only in the world of work but also, even more tellingly, in hazardous male-only endeavors such as warfare."[36]

Kelly sees, as does Cravey, that the economic shifts that began in the 1970s sharply unsettled preexisting gender arrangements. It was reasonable to expect that women as a group would gain greater autonomy and a more equitable footing with men when more women entered the formal labor force. This has been true in the United States, where the wage gap between men and women has decreased, but also in Mexican border cities, where "even the low pay earned by women in the maquiladoras has offered them a modicum of independence." However, in both poor and rich countries, "the new premises surrounding gender have paralleled devastating assaults on workers of both sexes."[37] Kelly points out that a significant part of the decrease in wage differentials in the United States is due to a decline in men's wages. In this chapter, we have examined the effects of the assault on Mexican workers.

My analysis of current systems of food and apparel production points to the need for systemic transformation of the political economy for justice to prevail. There are no individual solutions. As long as capital and transnational corporations are free to roam the globe in search of cheap labor and lax labor and environmental laws, we are caught up in a "race to the bottom." The rules of the game must change. Chapters 4 and 5 will discuss movements for social justice, locally and globally. But first I want to address a question asked by Christians in developing nations, "Why are the North American churches so silent about the evils of global capitalism?" and how that might change.

Questions for Discussion

1. Think about what you have eaten and worn for the last day or so. What parts of the world have your food and clothes come from? Do you know anything about the conditions under which they were produced?

2. Discuss the "McDonaldization" of the work force. What do you see as the strengths and weaknesses of this model from a social and economic standpoint?

3. What is a sweatshop? Do you think that sweatshop conditions should be ended in the United States? Abroad? What are your reasons for your view?

4. Wal-Mart is the world's largest retailer, with annual sales in excess of $138 billion—more than the total GNP of many poor countries. Do you think that Wal-Mart's contracting

and employee policies are fair? What are your reasons for your view?

Additional Resources

Barndt, Deborah, ed. *Women Working the NAFTA Food Chain: Women, Food and Globalization.* Toronto: Second Story Press, 1999. An interesting collection of essays from a collective of Canadian and Mexican women scholars and activists.

Bonacich, Edna, and Richard Appelbaum. *Behind the Label: Inequality in the Los Angeles Apparel Industry.* Berkeley: University of California Press, 2000. Although its focus is on Los Angeles, this book is an excellent analysis of the garment industry here and abroad.

THREE

What Does Faith
Have to Do with Globalization?

To kill the dream of a just and inclusive society is to entrap humanity
in the status quo, to render the power of religious imagination moot,
and to rob persons of hope and power to act for change.
—BEVERLY W. HARRISON,
"The Fate of the Middle 'Class' in Late Capitalism," 1991

Globalization, like slavery, is an oppressive system that denies people
of their right of economic and social independence, indeed their right
to life. Its commodification of life and its unethical measurement of
life only in economic parameters that sacrifice humanity at the altar
of profit cannot go unchallenged. Theology might not provide all the
answers in the fight against globalization but it can provide the social
framework within which to offer alternative, ethical responses to the
process.
— Young African Theologians' Statement, Accra, Ghana, October 2000

I believe that channels of grace are accessible through *conscious* experience of economic and ideological captivity that is acknowledged,
shared, and analyzed.
— BARBARA RUMSCHEIDT, *No Room for Grace*, 1998

Shortly after I returned from the Borderlinks trip to Mexico in
the fall of 2000, I heard a woman who had attended the 1999
International Missiology Conference repeat a question asked there:
"Why are the North American churches so silent about the evils
of global capitalism?" The question certainly resonated with my
own experiences in Mexico, and in Africa the year before. I had
seen some of these evils and had heard poignant stories of suffering and injustice. Why, I too have wondered, are people of good
will—religious and secular—silent in the face of these injustices?

63

Of course, there are those Christians who do not see corporate-ruled global capitalism as evil. For example, the Rev. Lou Sheldon, chair of the Traditional Values Coalition, believes that churches have a vested interest in keeping factories like those in Saipan open (see chapter 2). He sees this as a great opportunity to preach to people from countries, such as China, that make it difficult for evangelists to preach there. He claims that when the workers return to their countries, they will not only have money, but also will be full of faith.[1]

Still, there are many Christians who recognize the injustice within corporate-ruled global capitalism and remain silent. Have we given up the dream of a just and inclusive society? Have we closed our eyes and ears to people crying out for justice?

As I pondered these questions as the theme of a sermon I was to preach, I found that the parable of the sower (Mark 4:3–8) provides a biblical lens for identifying some crucial factors in this silence. The parable is about a sower who scatters seeds, but only some yield a good harvest. After telling the parable, Jesus interprets it for his disciples (Mark 4:13–20). Some seeds "are sown among the thorns: these are the ones who hear the word, but the cares of the world, and the lure of wealth, and the desire for other things come in and choke the word, and it yields nothing" (Mark 4:18–19). Is this not what in North America "shuts our eyes" and makes "our ears hard of hearing?" I think so. But some of us may also be like the "ones sown on rocky ground ... who have no root and endure only for a while when trouble or persecution arises" (Mark 4:17). I am suggesting that we cannot bear to see and to hear suffering that arises from evil. It is painful, difficult, especially if we feel implicated in the forces that cause injustice and feel powerless to make needed change.

In this chapter, I examine ways that being caught in these forces—what Rumscheidt calls our "economic and ideological captivity"[2]—silences us because we literally cannot see. We have no critical vision. I explore spiritual and religious resources for the development of critical vision and voice to challenge forces of unjust economic globalization. I speak as a white, middle-stratum Euro-American Protestant woman, primarily addressing others like myself. I believe, though, that these are issues that many people of some privilege face. Others may recognize the captivity I explore and resonate with aspects of the spirituality of resistance and solidarity I articulate. Each section draws on both secular and Christian sources. I want to speak specifically about Christianity, but not just because this is my own religious tradition. The Christian church is a global institution, committed to an ethic of neighbor love. Thus, it could be a crucial force in the struggle for global social and economic justice.[3]

Sources of Silence

Since the question about silence was asked of the North American churches, some theologically informed readers might think that their silence is another instance of liberal Protestantism's accommodation to culture—to use H. Richard Niebuhr's categories.[4] I claim, rather, that this situation is constitutive of life in the turn-of-the-century United States. Liberal Protestants, Evangelicals, Fundamentalists, Pentecostals, Roman Catholics, people from other religions or no religion—*all are shaped by the cultural forces of global capitalism.* Two Christian ethicists, one drawing on the cultural theory of Raymond Williams, the other on the sociology of Pierre Bordieu, offer insight into this dynamic.

A Culture of Material Desire and Consumption

Mary McClintock Fulkerson traces the ways our desires and dispositions are channeled by the determinations of advanced global capitalism. She persuasively argues that we must take seriously "the fact that culture is a dynamic and circulating reality in the late-twentieth-century global capitalism; it is the production of everyday realities that cannot be escaped." It is within this specific context that we create our identities and projects. This is not "a neutral making of choice," but rather, a process that is shaped "through a priori cultural meanings that produce desire and pleasure." She refers to Lawrence Grossberg's notion of "mattering maps" to describe ways that "culture creates the things that matter for subjects." Because of the media of late-twentieth-century technologies, this culture is "everywhere disseminated in ways that confound the boundaries of church, neighborhood, and nation. There is no personal identity or commodity that does not have attached to it associations that provoke and channel desire."[5] I think of, for instance, the recent launching of magazines dedicated to simplicity. The one I subscribed to mixed articles of a spiritual bent with others featuring very expensive clothing and furniture.

Ethicist Garth Kasimu Baker-Fletcher observes, "The socio-cultural milieu in which most Westerners have been raised—from the poorest to the richest, no matter what subcultural ethnicity, race, or color—has produced a macro-habitus of material desire, the inculcation of a fierce competitiveness to accumulate capital of all forms." This has led to "an unforeseen devaluing of human dignity and labor in favor of maximizing monetary profit by any means necessary." He notes that although different values may be held in what can be called the micro-habitus of family, "the macro-habitus of consumptive, competitive, materialist hedonism has severely restricted the moral vision of *all* Western nations and peoples and constricted our ethical capacities to grapple effectively with global problems of hunger, poverty, and environmental destruction."[6] Certainly, advertising, which costs nearly $200 billion a year in the United States, plays a crucial role in stoking material desire. But it is not the only significant factor.

In his eloquent *Spirituality of Resistance,* philosopher, ethicist and activist Roger Gottlieb offers psychosocial insight into the ecological crisis that is relevant to our discussion. Gottlieb charges that government, media, and schools do not really talk very much about environmental issues; and when they do, the conversation is often superficial. Thus, it is difficult for people to be informed about the environment, or hunger or poverty. He insightfully describes how consumption becomes "a measure of public identity," and how work is used "to fill the void left by a lack of community." He suggests that this is particularly true for those in the middle class, who have neither immense wealth nor the close ties of some lower economic groups. Work becomes "the core of our attempt to feel that we are significant." In meeting these perceived needs for identity and meaning in this way, "we ally ourselves with the dominant institutions of society. *Thrown into a social world we have not chosen, we are dependent on it for a sense of identity and validation.*"[7] This is, I think, a fitting contemporary analysis of what the parable of the sower describes as "the ones who hear the word, but the cares of the world, and the lure of wealth, and the desire for other things come in and choke the word, and it yields nothing" (Mark 4:18–19).

Denial and Avoidance

In my own work for sexual, racial, and economic justice, I have found that denial and avoidance are coping strategies we often use when faced with injustice and evil, whether personal or systemic.[8] Gottlieb describes ways we avoid or deny our implication in environmental destruction. For example, we say that problems like global warming are not as bad as they seem. Or we believe that science and technology will solve these problems, even though "governmental and corporate interests determine the direction and content of research." Or we hide the truth that is known, perhaps by foisting dangers like toxic waste off on communities of poor people of color. Gottlieb charges that this is a spiritual problem, because *spiritual development requires that we see things for what they are.* "As avoidance leads to the repression of energy, denial cuts us off from the truth, makes us doubt our own sense of how things are, keeps us from listening to others or the world and from changing the way things are."[9] We *all* pay a high price for denial and avoidance.

One way for those who do catch a glimpse of painful realities to avoid and deny is to plead innocence. When I first heard the question about the silence of the North American churches, that was one of my responses. I wanted to believe that I was not guilty of this charge, because I do speak out about economic injustice. I am part of a Christian organization that does. Although there is truth in my claim, I realized that even so, I am part of the North American churches, so I cannot so easily shift all responsibility from myself. (Sometimes people do this by blaming government, even though we who are citizens are part of government.) In a similar way, I must not think that practices like recycling relieve me of responsibility for the ecological crisis.

Pastoral theologian Barbara Rumscheidt thinks that white Anglo-Saxon Protestants especially have been "nurtured in innocence, in habits of avoidance and denial." She suggests that the *collective* identity of this group "has been shaped by tactful silence and discreet euphemism concerning historical connections between Christian mission, colonialism, capitalism, and racism"—or, one might add, the churches' silence in the face of the monstrous African slave trade, which young African theologians recently recalled in their recent visit to Elmina slave castle in Ghana (built in 1482 by the Portuguese, it has a church as its center.)

Rumscheidt writes that those of us in this group must let go of "a conditioned good conscience" in order to develop "critical consciousness," the ability to see clearly. This does not need to be a cause of despair, though. She believes that "channels of grace are accessible through *conscious* experience of economic and ideological captivity that is acknowledged, shared, and analyzed."[10] This point will be discussed in the next section.

Yet another avoidance strategy in the face of socioeconomic inequality is to offer explanations for one's privilege. Drawing on Max Weber, French sociologist Pierre Bordieu claims, "Dominant groups always need a 'theodicy of their own privilege,' or more precisely, a sociodicy, in other words a theoretical justification of the fact that they are privileged." He suggests that "competence is nowadays at the heart of that sociodicy."[11] In my experience, merit is the concept used in the United States. Those of us in dominant groups try to justify our privilege by claiming that we have earned it through competence or merit. The obvious corollary is that less privileged groups are not competent, or do not merit "rewards" that the privileged earn.

Understandings of the Core Vision of Christianity

Some people, both within and without churches, think that legally churches should not speak about public policy. They interpret the two religion clauses of the U.S. Constitution's First Amendment, the second of which came to be called "separation of church and state," to mean that the church cannot speak on matters of state or public policy. I find such arguments unpersuasive.[12]

Some Christians are silent about the global economy because they do not see matters of politics and economics as part of the "core vision" of Christianity. They are concerned that statements on these matters might detract from that vision. Robert Benne, a prominent voice from within the Lutheran tradition, is a good example of this position. Benne claims that the calling of the church "is to proclaim and gather a people around the gospel, forming them through the Spirit into the body of Christ."[13] He believes that Christianity has both a core religious vision and a core moral vision. The religious vision is centered on the event of Jesus as the Christ and is well summarized in the ecumenical creeds. The moral vision is expressed in the Decalogue (Ten Commandments), a calling to faith active in love and justice, the preciousness of all life redeemed by Christ, and the covenantal structure of God's creation (which includes the special covenant of man and woman in marriage).

Beyond that are "more speculative theological reflections of the church, including its social teachings" on economics, politics, and society. Benne affirms the importance of such "ventures," but since unanimity on them is unlikely, he believes that the church needs to allow "a good deal of latitude for disagreement and plurality of opinions" and must not let what he calls "extensions" conflict with the core vision itself. Only in special times on special issues (which he does not identify) should the church stand for or against specific public policy issues.[14]

I will discuss religious and moral vision in the next section, but I do want to point out here that Benne seems to be assuming that the core vision, or our interpretation of it, has not been shaped by culture—politics, economics, or society. Three decades of feminist scholarship have worked to uncover how hierarchical, patriarchal structures and worldviews shaped scripture and tradition, including the ecumenical creeds.[15] Of particular interest to me is that in speaking of the core moral vision, Benne does not specify what form(s) love and justice might take, but privileges marriage when speaking of covenants. Certainly, theological and biblical reasons exist for making such claims. But I contend that there are strong scriptural warrants to claim that the option for the poor and oppressed—social justice—is central to the moral vision of both the First and Second Testaments, whereas marriage is not.[16]

Others, including Lutheran biblical scholar Wolfgang Stegemann, claim that our attitude toward the poor is a matter of faith itself. In other words, he challenges the separation that Benne makes between the religious and moral core visions. Stegemann declares,

The relationship of Christians, churches, and theologians to global poverty no longer concerns merely Christianly self-evident charitable practice; it is becoming, rather, a question of Christian self-understanding. At issue is not merely a practical *consequence* of our faith in the saving revelation of God in Jesus Christ; *at issue is this faith itself.* The parable of the great judgment in Matt. 25:31–46 indicates the direction: our relationship to the poor of this world and our relationship to Jesus Christ, the Son of Man, are one and the same thing.[17]

These are matters we will explore in more depth in the next section.

As we do that, we must keep in mind some cautions from Mary McClintock Fulkerson, whose explanations about the way culture shapes our "mattering maps" began this section. She warns that because of this dynamic, we cannot discuss Christian discourse and practice "apart from the social formations of the state, civil society and economy, and its intersection by global capitalism and its cultural formations." Nor can we "assume that Christians can efface or transform the effects of these social forces with their ideas." Drawing again on Williams, she claims, "The effects of late global capitalism have penetrated so completely into the daily practices of life that only an alternative cultural formation can resist."[18] How might we—both secular and religious people—begin to create such a cultural formation?

Sources of Resistance and Solidarity

"A spirituality of resistance," Gottlieb claims, "marries traditional religious ideas of moral concern with social awareness. In an ecocidal age, that awareness will see the suffering not just of my neighbor, but of the whole world, and will extend itself to the nonhuman as well as the human." Gottlieb points out that to resist is "to seek an essential change in how we produce, distribute, and consume. A real solution will require that we alter our most basic ideas about what is important and what we want for our children." This is an immense challenge.[19]

Raising Awareness

Gottlieb is concerned to develop a spirituality that brings inner peace even with the overwhelming ecological destruction we face. He believes that this is possible only as we move from avoidance and denial to resistance. Referring to his insight about too many finding identity through work and thus dominant institutions, he suggests that "resistance is a way to have an identity that gives meaning without being a slave to the institutional identities that pollute and destroy." To do this, we must separate what is of ultimate value for us from what is considered "success."[20]

> The particular content of this identity may be described as a humble, compassionate sense of morality, as a genuine, selfless political solidarity, or as a pursuit of a spiritual Inner Truth. How we describe it is not important. What counts is that this identity enables us to be free of the seductive, addictive need for the approval of a society that is capable of destroying the earth.[21]

Resistance leads to peace because "all the psychic energy that had been trapped by denial, avoidance, hopeless despair, untrammeled grief, or submissive waiting" is freed. Finally, Gottlieb claims that "our own spiritual life can reach its most profound point when we join our energies with people around the world who are resisting environmental destruction."[22]

Rumscheidt is concerned with the dehumanization caused by the global economy. To resist it, she contends that "we must apprehend and comprehend the harm it causes" (tasks we have undertaken in the first two chapters). Although this can be a painful process, Rumscheidt believes that "channels of grace are available when we acknowledge, share and analyze our ideological and economic captivity." This requires bringing to the surface what she calls "internalized blocks to redemptive knowing," including "fear of dehumanization (one's own and others'), strategies of denial and evasion, and counterfeits of well-being"[23]—such as those described by Gottlieb.

One form dehumanization can take is "de-emotionalization," what I call numbing. I agree with Rumscheidt that "hearing through others' ears and seeing through others' eyes is a critically redeeming faith response" to this form of dehumanization. "We discover, or recover by rediscovery, an original sense of covenant connection, as a real and redeeming alternative to competitive, adversarial relationships." This creates "critical faith experience of the actual possibility of humanization." This becomes a new logic, over against the logic of dehumanization.[24]

The Biblical Narrative

For Fulkerson, one way to develop resistance is through communities "guided by a Jesus narrative with a syntax of solidarity with the Other." However, she cautions that "what cannot be determined in advance if we take cultural materialism seriously is the critical force of the biblical narrative," for the imagined communities or worlds we all inhabit are already shaped by interpretations of others and the "corresponding social relations." For instance, she critiques postliberal theological commitment to masculine images in biblical texts about Jesus. Similarly, I critiqued Benne's privileging of the creeds with their hierarchical, masculine imagery. Fulkerson is concerned that there be resistance "to the imagined community of the nation and its gender, class and race blindness." I want to facilitate resistance to the imagined community of the global economy, which, as the young African theologians so vividly claim, "sacrifices humanity at the altar of profit." We need readings of the Jesus narrative that do not reinscribe sexism, racism, or classism, but rather, nurture feelings of solidarity, which enable resistance to the logic of profit before all else and generate yearnings for social, economic, and ecological justice.[25]

Such a reading is one that foregrounds Jesus' proclamation of the "kin-dom,"[26] or *basileia*. Susan Brooks Thistlethwaite and Peter Crafts Hodgson offer a compelling reading:

> In his parables Jesus envisioned this basileia as essentially communal and social: it was an image of a new way of being human in the world in relation to God and neighbor that broke the logic of the old world and of ordinary human relationships under the sway of domination and control, reward and punishment. God's rule called forth a new human com-

munity, a communion of love, of liberation, of inclusion, of gratuity, of equality.

The basileia vision implied a radical alteration in social and institutional structures, and indeed Jesus himself put this vision into practice by gathering a network of disciples that was open to all without any prior conditions or privileges and that sharply challenged traditional social divisions and stratifications. Ultimately he died because of the severe threat his message and movement posed to the established authorities.[27]

Of the many parables that envision a new logic, three will illustrate the point. The parable of the last judgment" (Matt. 25:31–46), cited above by Stegemann, develops the logic of solidarity with the hungry, naked, stranger, and imprisoned. The parable of the good Samaritan (Luke 10:25–37) turns upside down narrow notions of neighbor so that the despised other becomes the exemplary neighbor. The parable of the laborers in the vineyard (Matt. 20:1–16), where all receive the same daily wage (about enough to feed a family for a day) regardless of when they began working, challenges the logic of merit and reward that undergirds the global economy.[28]

The Jesus narrative draws on prophetic and wisdom traditions from Hebrew scripture.[29] The prophetic is evident, for instance, in Luke's Gospel, when Jesus begins his ministry by reading in the synagogue from the prophet Isaiah: "The Spirit of the Lord is upon me, because he has anointed me to bring good news to the poor. He has sent me to proclaim release to the captives and recovery of sight to the blind, to let the oppressed go free, to proclaim the year of the Lord's favor" (Luke 4:18–19).

Social justice is seldom seen as a concern of wisdom literature. However, Bruce V. Malchow points out in his review of this literature that in teaching about "the needy," justice is mentioned more than charity. Justice rather than charity was understood to be a more basic need of the deprived. Many in Israel were poor because they had been cheated, for instance by being deprived of their property or a just wage. (We have seen that this is true today, too.) Therefore, the wise respond to a basic social need in calling for justice for the poor. "Minimally showing justice to the poor means not maltreating them as others do." But "the counsel of the wise goes beyond not doing wrong. It also calls for the active doing of right." Malchow shows that Qoheleth, the teacher also known as Ecclesiastes, denies the legitimacy of retribution theory, which states that those who suffer do so because they have sinned. In Qoheleth's time, as in ours, some privileged people use this theory to justify their privilege.[30] A careful reading of such literature, including the book of Job, might lead us to reconsider our sociodicy of merit.

Jesus' teachings and parables also challenged the conventional wisdom that we suffer because we sin, and offered instead the alternative wisdom—the radical, inclusive love—of God's kin-dom. Jesus also warned that we cannot serve both God and wealth (Matt. 6:24). In her study of wealth in the New Testament, Sondra Ely Wheeler concludes, "Taken with any degree of seriousness, the ideas that possessions are quite likely to defeat the desire to follow Christ or that the natural norm for deciding what to keep and what to give away is that the needs of all in the community be met equally have the potential to remake the material lives of affluent modern Christians in a fundamental way."[31]

The Call to Conversion

This is a call to conversion, a "turning away from" to "turning toward"—away from desire for wealth and status toward social justice and inclusive love. Communities shaped by these narratives could develop a "structure of feeling" to turn from the yearnings of rampant consumerism and other destructive forces of corporate-led globalization toward the desire of enough for all, human and nonhuman. As Mary Hobgood says, this requires "that we think differently about our world and our place in it."[32] We might call this an epistemological conversion, in which we turn from individualism and narrow notions of community toward a relational self in a radically imagined inclusive community of all living things.

These turns are crucial to resisting the desires that choke the word of the kin-dom—to use the images from the parable of the sower. However, we may still face difficult spiritual challenges. Will we endure when trouble or persecution arises? We may yearn for enough for all and participate in communities that practice social justice and inclusive love, but anyone who is socially and ecologically aware knows that we are still caught in destructive and oppressive forces we cannot control. It is not possible to be righteous, if we understand righteousness to mean "clean hands and a pure heart"—an innocence we may deeply desire.[33] With Baker Fletcher, who describes ethics as engagement, we can see the moral task as getting our hands "dirty with life."

As we have previously noted, it is virtually impossible to survive—particularly for people of some privilege—without participating in systems of economic exploitation and ecological destruction. Besides, even if withdrawal from these systems were possible, it is not necessarily an effective way to struggle for social justice. This is also true of "voluntary simplicity" alternative lifestyles, which certainly have a place in helping us develop a sense of enough and reducing our burden on the planet. But these alone, in my judgment, do not begin to dismantle exploitative and oppressive structures and practices. Rumscheidt speaks of "channels of grace" being accessible when we realize our captivity. This brings to mind Martin Luther's notion that we are at the same time sinners yet justified (by grace). Although this foundational belief may be comforting, in practice it can seem rather abstract. Just what does it really mean? At worst, as Dietrich Bonhoeffer noted, grace can become cheap if we forget the call to discipleship.

The Practice of Accountability

I learned a practice from the Ecumenical Institute in Chicago that has been useful in facing this dilemma. I was a participant in the Institute's summer 1965 college program. We were asked to commit to a covenant grounded in biblical notions of love and justice during our summer together. Each week we held ourselves accountable to the covenant after a simple meal together. What struck me deeply was that we were encouraged not to answer yes or no, but either yes/no or no/yes (i.e., more or less faithful). This freed me from feelings of despair and worthlessness, knowing I likely would never be able to be completely faithful to our covenant. Yet I was still held accountable—no cheap grace here!

Each week during the summer I carefully reflected on whether I had been more, or less, faithful to our covenant. I have not been in a formally covenanted community like that since then, but I periodically hold myself accountable in this way to the real and imagined communities of which I am a part. Since by virtue of my social location I am part of the dominant privileged community, a vision of imagined communities with those who suffer oppression and exploitation is crucial to a spirituality of resistance and solidarity. These are the communities to whom I am accountable, while working for change in the dominant communities of which I am a part. For example, I might envision the women I met in Uganda or Mexico. Or I envision threads connecting me to the women and men from around the world who also participated in the United Nations Decade for Women Conference or the World Council of Churches Ecumenical Decade Conference, and from them to their communities, social and ecological. I am—we all are—part of webs of connection, whose nodes may represent those with whom we have had face-to-face dialogue, more personal connections. The challenge is to make this symbolic accountability real.[34]

A Theology of the Cross

Although these practices are an important part of my spirituality of resistance and solidarity, they alone have not been "the root" that makes endurance in the face of trouble or persecution possible (Mark 4:17). Hopelessness is often the most difficult spiritual challenge we face. How can we bear to really see and hear those whose suffering arises from evil, especially if we do not know a way to overcome the evil? What might be "the root" that would enable us to see, to hear? I propose that Christians consider a "theology of the cross." I know that many liberals and progressives like myself have been uncomfortable with the cross as it has been used by those who oppress and exploit to justify their actions. The cross has a long history of legitimating unnecessary suffering. Or, as Mary Daly charges, it is the symbol of a death-centered religion.[35]

There is much truth to these charges. But the cross is a symbol with surplus meaning. Feminist theologian Mary Solberg critically integrates feminist epistemology and Luther's theology of the cross to develop an epistemology of the cross. This is "an attempt to describe, not explain, how God's solidarity with the world underwrites our own solidarity with those on the margins." For her, such an epistemology describes a shift in consciousness, and conscience, from the recognition "Everyone must be somewhere" (social location) to the question "Where must I be?" (moral accountability for social location).[36]

Solberg suggests that only a "privileged church" may need an epistemology of the cross, as only "a privileged church needs to come to terms with its illusions."[37] I have learned that the cross can help us see things as they are—the brokenness of a world that crucifies one who brings good news of God's just and inclusive kin-dom. Or, to borrow Martin Luther's concepts, over against a theology of glory that celebrates the triumph of global capitalism as if that meant the well-being of all peoples, a theology of the cross sees and hears those who suffer from its evils. The theology of the cross then leads to a theology of solidarity.[38]

We can learn from womanist theologian Joanne Terrell that "suffering points up the need for holiness, experienced as wholeness." For her, "Holiness is agency; it is spiritual power for enduring, resisting and overcoming the causes of suffering."[39] Emilie Townes, another womanist theologian and ethicist, asserts that "suffering is sinful because we do not choose to act through our finite freedom on behalf of our liberation from sin to injustice." God has spoken against injustice and evil, she reminds us, through the "the Suffering Servant." This resonates with Thistlethwaite and Hodgson's reading of the Jesus narrative, that he died because of the severe threat his message and movement posed to the established authorities.[40]

For Townes, the empty cross and tomb are symbols of the victory over evil and injustice. Her most important insight, in my judgment, is that it is not suffering itself that frees the oppressed to struggle against injustice, but "their pain that can be recognized and named as injustice and brokenness" (to use Rumscheidt's words, the apprehension and comprehension of evil by both the oppressed and oppressors, including those who recognize their own implication in systems of oppression). In Townes's view, "The resurrection moves humanity past suffering to pain and struggle... move[s] the person from victim to change agent."[41] This reading of the cross does not encourage passive acceptance of death, suffering, or injustice; it encourages agency, action, solidarity, accountability—a praxis of discipleship.

Feminist biblical interpreter and theologian Elisabeth Schüssler Fiorenza charges us in our reading of resurrection to look to the

empty tomb that the women found when they went to care for
Jesus' body. "The empty tomb does not signify absence but pres-
ence." The women at the tomb were told that "the Resurrected
One" would be present "on the road ahead, in a particular space
of struggle and recognition such as Galilee." We find "the Resurrected One ... present in the 'little ones' in the struggles for survival
of those impoverished, hungry, imprisoned, tortured, and killed, in
the wretched of the earth."[42]

Struggling for Social Justice

Such a reading speaks powerfully to the experiences of those of
us involved in social justice struggles. I think, for instance, of the
Borderlinks trip to Agua Prieta, Mexico. At the Holy Family Parish,
we heard the stories of workers struggling to protect their rights, like
getting legal severance pay when maquilas leave for countries with
even cheaper labor. "This work is a work of faith for us," we were
told by one woman, who explained that their reading of the gospel
developed their self-esteem and gave them the courage to struggle
for their rights. Another woman, encouraged by her coworkers, told
about turning down promotions and pay raises offered by management to move her out of the union, where she was an effective
leader. For her, this was not a sacrifice; solidarity is the path of
discipleship.

Feminist ethicist Beverly Harrison reminds us, "Without blessed
persistence, without the willingness to risk, even unto death, the
power of radical love would not live on in the world. There are no
ways around crucifixions, given the power of evil in the world."
Our aim is to bring an end to crucifixions "through actions of mu-
tuality and solidarity."[43] Such actions can sustain us in the face of
the overwhelming odds we face in our justice-making efforts.

The Zapatista uprising began on January 1, 1994, the launch
of the North American Free Trade Agreement, as a protest against
free trade and neoliberalism. Chase Manhattan Bank was concerned
enough about the effect of the Zapatista movement on investments
that it sent a memo to the Mexican government early in 1995
urging the use of armed force to destroy the Zapatistas.[44] A campaign of low-intensity conflict culminated in the Acteal massacre
on December 22, 1997, when forty-five Chiapans who supported

the Zapatista movement were massacred by paramilitaries who had links to the armed forces.

I participated in a demonstration in front of the Mexican consulate in Los Angeles a few months after the Acteal massacre in Chiapas, Mexico. This was sponsored by the National Commission on Democracy in Mexico (NCDM), the U.S. Zapatista solidarity group. As part of the action, Crystal Echohawk, a Native American who was part of the NCDM, would submit petitions with hundreds of signatures from around the United States to the consular officer, demanding that the rights of the indigenous peoples of Mexico be respected and that terror such as this massacre be ended. When we arrived at the demonstration, on Good Friday 1998, at the center of the space where we gathered was a large cross on which hung the effigy of a young indigenous woman with flowers around her neck. We were each given a cross with the name of one of the victims—mostly women and children—to hang around our necks until we stacked them together outside the consulate. The reality of the crucifixions caused by neoliberalism was powerfully present in our midst, yet our remembrance of these victims filled us with life and hope, not emptiness and death. As Harrison so eloquently tells us, there is a strength that shines forth in women's lives, in poor peoples' lives, even in the midst of terror.[45] This strength can empower us to continue the struggle for social justice, for a world where all may flourish.

The move from silence to speech to action will not be an easy one, as is evident from our examination of sources of silence. Yet, there are possibilities for a spirituality of resistance and solidarity. Gottlieb offers useful ways to develop such a spirituality, drawing on psychosociological insights and his own experience. His is a path open to all. I have drawn on Christian thinkers and my own experience to suggest ways that our faith sources can nurture communities of resistance and solidarity. In my own spiritual journey, Jesus is the one on the horizon, beckoning us toward fuller realization of God's just and inclusive kin-dom.

In her discussion of the biblical image of the New Jerusalem as a horizon, Emilie Townes suggests questions we must ask: What is the society we are trying to create? What does it look like? Is there a common vision? I propose that the global society we envision is one in which there is "sufficient, sustainable livelihood for all." This criterion from the Evangelical Lutheran Church in America's "Social Statement on Economic Life" is a useful alternative to the rapacious logic of economic globalization. It resonates with an embodied sense of resurrection and the principles of other denominations' social teaching; the World Council of Churches' vision of justice, peace, and the integrity of creation; and Jesus proclamation of "respect for the life of every being and abundant life for all."[46]

I will flesh out this vision in the following two chapters, returning to the case studies from chapters 1 and 2. I will explore justice-making movements—specifically Christian and coalitions of human rights, environmental, religious, labor, women's and other groups. There are movements that are making a difference in people's lives. Even so, the task before us can seem daunting. Latin American theologian Elsa Tamez draws on Ecclesiastes to offer words of wisdom at times when it seems that horizons are closing upon themselves: "affirming concrete life in the joy of eating bread, drinking wine, and enjoying life with the loved one." This, she says, is neither irresponsibility nor indifference in the face of exploitation. Rather, this is "a move for life because one rests under the grace of God, even in the midst of enslaving labor and its anti-human logic."[47]

The value of this became clear to me during the Ecumenical Decade of Women Conference. We had experienced emotionally wrenching sessions in which we heard firsthand accounts of exploitation, even death, from African women describing the impact of debt on their lives, and from women from around the world who had been victimized by sexual violence. Our global banquet and celebration, during which we sang and danced "We are marching in the light of God," was a grace-filled move for life. May this sense of grace continue with us as we turn to examine the struggles for abundant life for all.

Questions for Discussion

1. What do you see as sources of silence in your own life? Your group or community?

2. Do you agree with Barbara Rumscheidt that some of us need to let go of our "conditioned good conscience"? What are your reasons for your view?

3. What are some sources of resistance and solidarity in your life? Your group or community?

4. What does the cross symbolize to you? Do you think that a theology of the cross can lead to a theology of solidarity?

5. Discuss the usefulness of the ethical principle of sufficient, sustainable livelihood for all.

Additional Resources

van den Berg, Aart. *God and the Economy: Analysis and Typology of Roman Catholic, Protestant, Orthodox, Ecumenical and Evangelical Theological Documents on the Economy, 1979–92.* Delft: Eburon Publishers, 1998. Useful summaries and analysis of ecclesial statements as well as authors like Michael Novak and Ulrich Duchow.

Duchow, Ulrich. *Global Economy: A Confessional Issue for the Churches?* Geneva: World Council of Churches, 1987. A theological critique of capitalism.

Fiorenza, Elisabeth Schüssler. *In Memory of Her: A Feminist Theological Construction of Christian Origins.* New York: Crossroad, 1983. A classic text in feminist theology.

Gebara, Ivone. *Longing for Running Water: Ecofeminism and Liberation.* Minneapolis: Fortress Press, 1999. An important critical and constructive work.

Novak, Michael. *The Spirit of Democratic Capitalism.* New York: Simon and Schuster, 1983. A theological defense of capitalism.

Ruether, Rosemary Radford. *Sexism and God Talk: Toward a Feminist Theology.* Boston: Beacon Press, 1983. A classic text in Christian feminist theology.

Soelle, Dorothee. *On Earth as in Heaven: A Liberation Spirituality of Sharing.* Louisville: Westminster/John Knox Press, 1993. A moving collection of essays.

FOUR

What Can I Do?

I can begin to make food choices that break down the web of oppression.... I begin by choosing local produce, and when that is not available, I demand imported food that is grown in an ecologically appropriate, non-exploitative way.

—LAUREN BAKER, "A Different Tomato," 1999

That's why we organize the woman workers together and have them speak out their problems at each of the garment shops. If we stop being silent about these things, we can demand justice. We can get paid hourly, and bring better working conditions to the workers.

—LISA LIU, as told to David Bacon, 2000

It is time we reclaim the global economy for the people who make it work, and stop pandering to corporate interests who build their empires on the backs of the innocent.

—REP. CYNTHIA MCKINNEY,
United States Congress, 2000

In the conclusion to chapter 2, I claimed that an analysis of current systems of food and apparel production point to the need for systemic transformation of the political economy for justice to prevail. The rules of the game must change. In this chapter, I return to food and apparel production, as examples of how globalization impacts our daily lives, to discuss ways that individuals and groups, acting as consumers and citizens, can work for justice. I explore specific strategies, including solidarity campaigns in support of workers and/or unions, model legislation, and alternatives to these systems. The focus in this chapter is on local and regional efforts, some based in California, where much of the fresh produce in the United States is grown and a significant amount of mainland fashion is sewn. The next chapter will examine global movements. These movements together can be envisioned as part of what Jeremy Brecher and Tim

Costello call "the Lilliput strategy." Just as the Lilliputians immobilized the giant Gulliver with hundreds of tiny threads, so justice movements in different countries can employ a variety of tactics to restrain corporation-ruled globalization.[1]

How are these local and regional situations connected to globalization? In the first chapter, we examined some of the history of U.S.-Mexican relations as part of the development of international free trade agreements. In the second chapter, we explored the development of maquiladoras along the border after the United States ended its guestworker program for Mexican workers in 1965. In this chapter, we turn to the farmworker movement in the United States to explore the impact of those relationships and programs on this side of the border. When we turn to sweatshops in the garment industry, we need to broaden our view. Many of the people working in Los Angeles sweatshops have emigrated—with and without documents—from Central America and Asia. The civil wars in the 1980s—in El Salvador and Guatemala in particular—in which the United States played such a large role, created large refugee flows in the Central American region, with many people ending up in southern California.

Regional and global economic development strategies in the 1990s are also a significant factor. One can see, drawing on the work of Saskia Sassen and other scholars, that "the internationalization of capital" has contributed "to mobilizing people into migration streams." In particular, in third world countries the replacement of subsistence farming with export-oriented agriculture and manufacturing has helped push people out of their home countries. At the same time, "an international labor market for low-wage manual and service workers" has developed, with many of these jobs in first world countries and global cities around the world. This creates a pull for people to migrate to these cities or countries.[2]

Clearly, Los Angeles is one of these global cities. Los Angeles is increasingly multicultural, with over 260 languages spoken there. Its work force is one-third immigrant. The gap between the wealthy and the poor widens to a chasm. The wage structure is two-tiered: a small number of highly paid managerial and professional jobs along with a growing number of low-wage ones. These are characteristics of many global cities that are particularly pronounced in Los Angeles. The internationalization of capital and labor is the context for the "thousands of oppressive realities" we began to explore in chapter 2 and to which we return here. Sweatshop workers, whether in the fields or in garment factories, are at the intersection of structures of inequality based on racial/ethnic, gender, class, and national (immigrant or native) differences. These workers are among the most vulnerable—and most resilient.[3]

From "Grapes of Wrath" to Fruits of Justice

"Is there enough food for all?" I asked in the discussion of food production and distribution in chapter 2. The conclusion was that there is enough food for all, but too many people cannot afford it. In this section, I explore ways of responding to the "thousands of oppressive realities" in the food system we examined in chapter 2. John Hubner contends, "The degree of exploitation in the fields has always depended on the balance between workers and jobs."[4] When the guestworker program, started during World War II, ended in 1964, partly due to the efforts of the United Farm Workers (UFW), there were more jobs than workers for seven years. Cesar Chavez, Dolores Huerta, and the farmworker movement in the 1960s and 1970s inspired many Americans to reflect on how food got to our tables. A brief review of this history illustrates one effective way that people of conscience have participated in efforts to reduce exploitation of workers who help bring food to our tables: boycotts.

The Farmworker Movement

In 1965, a small group of farmworkers in California went on strike for a wage increase (from ninety cents an hour to $1.25). The National Farmworkers Association (later to become the United Farm Workers), cofounded by Chavez and Huerta in 1962, answered the call to support the striking workers. Chavez and Huerta had planned on a few more years of building the organization before striking; at the time of the 1965 strike there was only one hundred dollars in their bank account. Farmworkers and their supporters, like the National Farmworkers Ministry, traveled across the country telling about the poor wages and working conditions in the fields of California. Millions of people responded to the call to boycott table grapes, in support of the demand for successful negotiations. It was a long struggle (1967 to 1970), but eventually nearly all the growers did negotiate and sign contracts with the UFW. This was a significant accomplishment. Most people thought it would be impossible to organize migrant farmworkers. It came about through the leadership of Chavez, Huerta, and the workers themselves, supported by religious, labor, and social justice groups.[5] It was a hopeful time—part of the civil rights movement making changes across America.

A major challenge came, though, when the first contracts expired in 1973. Many growers refused to negotiate new contracts with the UFW, instead signing "sweetheart deals" with the Teamsters. The UFW called a second grape boycott, again traveling across the nation to gain support from consumers. This strike lasted until 1975. A Gallup poll at that time showed that seventeen million Americans were boycotting grapes. This boycott resulted in the enactment of the California Agricultural Labor Relations Act, the first law of its kind in the United States, which granted farmworkers the right to collectively organize and bargain for better wages and working conditions. (Agricultural workers are explicitly excluded from coverage under the U.S. National Labor Relations Act, and therefore have no federally guaranteed right of unionization and collective bargaining.) The UFW consequently won several elections and successfully negotiated contracts with grape, lettuce, and vegetable growers.

Another major challenge came in the early 1980s when newly elected California governor George Deukmejian, elected with strong support from growers, stopped enforcing the state's farm labor law. Thousands of farmworkers lost their UFW contracts; many were fired. Although the UFW regained some ground in the 1990s, many workers no longer receive the protection and benefits won by the UFW in this earlier period (see chapter 2). Reflecting on this situation gives us pause, reminding us of how difficult it can be to sustain the gains made in the struggle for economic justice, particularly for the most vulnerable workers. We also learn that changing the rules to be more just is not enough; the new rules must be enforced.

Yet, even here, there have been gains. In November 2000, the UFW called off its sixteen-year California table grape boycott targeting the use of dangerous pesticides, which Chavez called "The

Grapes of Wrath." UFW president Arturo Rodriguez said, "Cesar Chavez's crusade to eliminate use of five of the most toxic chemicals plaguing farmworkers and their families has been largely successful." In the same article in the *Los Angeles Times* that quoted Rodriguez, James Rainey reported, "Three pesticides that most concerned Chavez—Dinoseb, parathion and Phosdrin—are no longer used in the fields. A fourth pesticide, methyl bromide, is to be phased out and a fifth, Captan, is under much greater restriction."[6] While growers claimed that the UFW called off the boycott because it was not hurting their business, the elimination of these pesticides is an important victory. However, a report from the Pesticide Action Network North America cautions that enforcement of existing law needs to be strengthened. In particular, "California's Department of Pesticide Regulation (DPR) should abolish the option of issuing notices of violation that carry no fine, set minimum mandatory penalties, increase fine levels for moderate and serious violations, and abolish leniency toward violators who claim to be unfamiliar with regulatory requirements."[7] Farmworker access to medical treatment needs to be improved, and both farmworkers' and the public's right to know of pesticide danger and use ensured.

Governmental Responses

Human Rights Watch (HRW) points to other important justice issues in a recent report on child farmworkers, and also details recommended governmental responses. Hundreds of thousands of children and teens work in fields, orchards, and packing sheds across the United States. Under federal law, a twelve-year-old child could legally harvest asparagus or some other crop from 3 a.m. to 8 a.m., seven days a week, but be prohibited from working in most any nonagricultural work. Or a fifteen-year-old could work fifty hours a week during the school year in agriculture, but only eighteen hours a week in a fast-food business. They found that "agricultural work is the most hazardous and grueling area of employment open to children in the United States," as well as the least protected.[8]

HRW recommends several changes to U.S. law—changing the rules—to address these injustices. History indicates progressive legislation such as HRW recommends will not be passed without strong support from citizens, acting through various advocacy groups—faith-based, labor, human rights, and coalitions like those that earlier supported the UFW. A key change recommended by HRW is "that Congress amend the Fair Labor Standards Act (FLSA) to protect all working children equally. This means imposing, for the first time ever, limits on the number of hours children aged fifteen and younger can work in agriculture when school is in session." If such laws are passed, effective enforcement will be critical. Penalties for violating existing laws are low enough that some growers say, "The fine is only $1,000; I'll just pay it and keep doing things as I am."

In the U.S. House of Representatives, Rep. Tom Lantos (D-Calif.) has for the past twelve years introduced the "Young American Workers' Bill of Rights." The bill is widely supported by children's advocates. HRW points out, "It would enhance protection for many working children, including children working in agriculture." Because children work to help meet their families' basic needs, HRW argues, "Congress and the administration must acknowledge that farmworker families need assistance on all fronts. Enforcement of workers' rights, assurance of adequate housing, increased availability of traditional and nontraditional education, free and accessible health care, and other assistance as necessary—these are the minimum conditions necessary to ensure that all children in the United States, including the children of agricultural laborers, have the possibility of a safe, dignified, and healthy start in life."[9]

HRW describes two strategies used by government agencies, such as the Wage and Hour Division (WHD), to enforce labor law in agriculture, strategies that are also used in apparel production. One is to use the Fair Labor Standards Act's "hot goods" provision, which "prohibits the shipment in interstate commerce of any goods produced in violation of minimum wage, overtime, or child labor requirements." This provision can be very effective, particularly in agriculture, where products have a very short life span. It allows the WHD to seek temporary restraining orders preventing the movement of "tainted goods." Understandably, there is a strong incentive for growers and other affected businesses to cooperate with the WHD, because losing their crop is much more expensive than paying a fine. Forms of cooperation include future compliance agreements and provisions for ongoing monitoring.

A second strategy addresses the use of contractors by growers, who then claim that they are not responsible for violations of the law. WHD can find "joint employment—and therefore joint liability—between the grower and the farm labor contractor." WHD just recently started using this strategy in the farmworker context. Joint employment is determined "by looking at a variety of factors, including: whether the grower has the authority to control, either directly or indirectly, the workers or the work they perform; whether the grower has control over employment conditions or wage payment; and whether the work performed is an integral part of the grower's business." This strategy is important not only in challenging sweatshop conditions, but also in addressing injustices that arise in the growing casualization of labor in the global economy—what Pierre Bordieu calls "flexploitation."[10]

Consumer and Citizen Actions

In addition to solidarity actions with union organizing and negotiations though boycotts and advocacy of progressive labor legislation and enforcement, there are other kinds of consumer and citizen actions to resist injustices in the food production and distribution system. These tend toward developing alternatives to the conventional production and distribution systems. One promising strategy is "community-supported agriculture," a growing movement in Japan, Britain, and the United States. Daniel Imhoff identifies three goals farmers can achieve through this development: "mutually beneficial relationships with a community of consumers; environmentally sustainable farming practices; and public education on contemporary agricultural issues."[11]

Both farmers and consumers benefit from these arrangements, which ensure production of locally or regionally grown, high-quality food products. In Japan, where the movement began, it's called "farming with a face on it." I became aware of this movement through members of a local Unitarian-Universalist congregation, who arrange with a local organic farmer to purchase his produce for at least one growing season. These arrangements are usually called subscriptions. The farmer is assured of a market for his products and the purchasers of high quality, locally grown produce. In some cases, subscribers make partial payments at the beginning of the growing season, which saves the farmer the cost of borrowing to cover his production costs. Savings on marketing and transportation help keep the cost of food affordable and reduce negative environmental impacts.[12]

A similar approach to community-supported agriculture addresses the issue of those who cannot afford to purchase high-quality food, or at times even low-cost food. In fact, some of these programs incorporate this concern into their planning. For instance, the Homeless Garden Project in Santa Cruz, California, is committed to making jobs and nourishment available to homeless people in the city. MANNA, a food program in Nashville, provides coupons for produce from local organic farmers as part of its support of low-income families.[13]

Foodshare Toronto aims "to develop social policy and community projects that will alleviate the growing problem of urban hunger," according to its director, Debbie Fields. This group believes that "the current global food system isn't working very well to eliminate hunger or to promote optimum health." They are considering advocating that basic healthy foods be "outside fluctuating market relations," either through marketing boards that would set stable prices for farmers and consumers, or through government subsidies of basic foods. "Because of the potential benefits of using some market and cash means to help people express both personal choice and responsibility, we are particularly intrigued by models in which foods are available at wholesale prices, rather than free, to the entire population through government-subsidized community-based mechanisms." An interesting aspect of their position is that this is in part a public health issue, since diet is a significant risk factor in a great number of diseases.[14] This reminds us of how interrelated these issues are.

No Sweat:
Ending Injustice in Apparel Production

In the analysis of the system of apparel production in chapter 2, we also discovered many oppressive realities that need to be addressed. In this section, I explore strategies used by the antisweatshop movement to end sweatshop abuses in California and around the world.

As in the previous section, these include consumer and citizen actions. We begin with the movement that grew out of the 1995 El Monte incident described in chapter 2. A primary focus of its efforts has been to establish retail accountability.

Sweatshop abuses have increased dramatically in the last few decades, in part because of the practice of contracting and subcontracting by garment manufacturers and retailers. As we have seen, this is one practice corporations use to externalize risks and avoid responsibility for workers in the face of growing global competition. Contractors, who employ most of the workers, are squeezed by large chain retailers to lower their costs so that the retailers can raise their profit margin. The retailers then claim that they are not responsible for sweatshops, since they do not directly employ the workers. (Note the similarity to growers' claims discussed in the previous section.)

The antisweatshop movement believes that retailer accountability for wages and working conditions is key to stopping sweatshop abuses. Many retailers design the garments and buy the fabric, which they own throughout the sewing process. They set the amount they will pay contractors, who are much less powerful than retailers. Thus, they are the ones ultimately responsible for wages and working conditions.

Legal Actions

In some situations, lawsuits have successfully made this case. I will describe two important ones. Both were brought by groups that look to people of conscience for support of their work. The first was in regard to the 1995 El Monte, California, incident, where some seventy workers were found virtually enslaved in a garment factory. The U.S. government successfully brought criminal charges against most of the people who smuggled in the young women and kept them virtually enslaved. But that case did not cover the back wages owed the workers.

The Asian Pacific American Legal Center brought a civil case against manufacturers and retailers for whom the apparel was produced. This was a challenging case, because APALC had to pierce "the veil of corporate invisibility." This is a name for the legal doctrine that holds that contractors alone are responsible for wages and working conditions, not manufacturers or retailers. APALC brought suit on behalf of the Thai workers as well as a smaller group of Latino workers who were employed in the contractor's "front" operation. They successfully established that the manufacturers and retailers were responsible for back wages, because they owned the design and fabrics throughout the production process. Additionally, APALC showed that these parties had to know that illegal production was involved, since there was no way the workers in the front operation could have turned around orders in such a short time. The workers received $2 million in back wages and overtime.[15]

Lawsuits were also successful in establishing retailer accountability for production in Saipan (an island in the Marianas, a U.S. commonwealth) with a $1 billion garment industry. The Marianas are permitted by the U.S. government to control their own minimum wage, and immigration laws. Thousands of garment workers work and live there in deplorable conditions, putting in twelve to eighteen hours a day and earning $2.90 or less an hour. Most of the workers are young women recruited from China and the Philippines, who pay a cash bond of up to $5,000 for a one-year contract to work in a garment factory. Many of their contracts include clauses that restrict them from joining unions, attending religious services, quitting, or marrying. These practices are in violation of U.S. labor law and human rights. Yet, the apparel made there is shipped to the mainland, with no tariffs or quota restrictions, and it carries the coveted "Made in the USA" label.

In January 1999 three lawsuits were filed against eighteen U.S. clothing companies for mistreatment of workers in foreign-owned factories operating on U.S. soil. "These companies are accused of violating federal law by engaging in a 'racketeering conspiracy' using indentured labor to produce clothing on the island of Saipan. Their foreign owned garment contractors are also charged with failing to pay overtime and ongoing intolerable working and living conditions." Two are federal class-action lawsuits filed on behalf of more than fifty thousand workers. A third lawsuit was brought by Sweatshop Watch, Global Exchange, the Asian Law Caucus, and the Union of Needletrades, Industrial and Textile Employees (UNITE). Several retailers have settled this lawsuit, agreeing to independent monitoring of standards to end the worst abuses and ensure that factories adhere to U.S. and Saipan labor law, as well as legally required payments to workers. As of this writing, both The Gap and Target Corporation have refused to settle, so the coalition continues to pressure them to do so through telephone and letter campaigns, as well as demonstrations at some of their store locations.[16]

Other strategies for establishing retailer accountability are varied, depending in part on the context. These options include citizen, consumer, and investment actions. An individual might want to boycott retailers known to use sweatshops, but this could be difficult since so many retailers do. Organized campaigns are more likely to be effective. For instance, a holiday consumer campaign a few years ago against The Gap for its sweatshop production in El Salvador produced an agreement for independent monitoring of its factories there. (People of Faith Network played a crucial role in reaching this agreement.)[17] Concerned persons should learn about these solidarity campaigns and choose one or more to participate in and support financially.

Legislation

Legislation is a crucial strategy in establishing retailer accountability. In 1999, California passed AB 633—the strongest antisweatshop law in the United States—which provides that manufacturers and retailers pay workers minimum wage and overtime compensation when contractors they use fail to do so. The law also increases penalties for labor law violations and increases law enforcement activities. Rojana Chuenchujit, one of the enslaved El Monte workers, played a leadership role in the movement supporting passage of the legislation. She testified before the Assembly Committee on Labor and Employment and spoke at rallies in support of the legislation: "I get angry because people don't understand that we have to fight so hard to win our rights in this country."[18] Some retailers are now asking the governor for exemption from this law. Sweatshop Watch has organized a campaign to demand that the governor uphold the law and not give exemptions to corporations that want to evade their legal—and moral—responsibility. They have also established a Garment Workers Center to educate workers about their rights under the law.[19]

Clearly, enforcement of existing labor law as well as legislation establishing a degree of retailer accountability are effective means of reducing sweatshop abuses in the United States. But what about all that apparel—over one-half—produced outside the United States? Rep. Cynthia McKinney (D-Ga.) has introduced the Corporate Code of Conduct Act (H.R. 4596), which would require "all U.S.-based corporations with more than 20 employees abroad to enact a code of conduct" that would apply to its "subsidiaries, subcontractors, affiliates, joint ventures, partners, or licensees." The Code would mandate that companies in their overseas operations "pay a living wage and ban specific practices, such as mandatory overtime for workers under 18, pregnancy testing and retaliation against whistleblowers; respect identified international labor standards (including the right to organize, minimum wage guarantees and protections for occupational safety and health); adhere to both international environmental standards and U.S. federal environmental laws and regulations." Companies would have "to provide public documentation of where they are doing business directly or through subsidiaries or contractors, and extensive information on employment and environmental practices." Enforcement would be through (1) preference from the U.S. government to corporations in compliance with the Code in both contracts and export assistance, and (2) "victims of violations of the bill—including non-U.S. citizens—would be empowered to sue U.S. companies in U.S. courts." Although there is no likelihood of such a bill being passed by Congress in the near future, it does provide a basis for advocacy.[20]

A few cities, including San Francisco, Cleveland, Pittsburgh, and New York, have adopted procurement policies, which require companies producing uniforms and other products for the city to comply with a code of conduct. Citizens in other cities—and states—could organize for adoption of such policies. United Students Against Sweatshops (USAS) has been the most successful movement to date in establishing corporate accountability through procurement policies. USAS chapters around the country, through petitions, demonstrations, and sit-ins, have taken important steps in ensuring that the apparel bearing their school logos is not produced in sweatshop conditions.[21]

These and other efforts helped clarify the three key elements of an effective policy. The first is that retailers—or licensees, in the case of universities—must disclose the names and locations of their subcon-tractors. This is crucial if actual conditions are to be documented. Companies claimed that they could not do this because it would harm their competitive advantage. USAS, in successfully demand-ing that Nike disclose its contractors, was instrumental in exposing the hollowness of this claim. However, few companies have fol-lowed suit. The demand for disclosure is still an important goal of the antisweatshop movement. (The work of Charles Kernagan of the National Labor Committee has been crucial in documenting sweatshop conditions, particularly in Central America and Asia.)

The other two elements are a meaningful code of conduct and effective monitoring. These elements also continue to be areas of controversy. The primary example is the Fair Labor Association (FLA) Code of Conduct, produced by the White House Apparel Industry Partnership (AIP). This is a task force created by Presi-dent Clinton and Secretary of Labor Robert Reich in 1996, and is made up of companies, trade unions, and human rights and reli-gious groups. When FLA was formed by a subcommittee of AIP in late 1998, two unions—UNITE and the Retail, Wholesale and Department Store Union—and the Interfaith Center for Corporate Responsibility refused to sign the agreement because they believed it was biased in favor of the companies.

The FLA code does not mandate a living wage, allows excess overtime (a sixty- to seventy-hour week is permissible), and does not adequately uphold workers' rights to organize independent unions. Also, it does not require full public disclosure of factories, making independent monitoring impossible. When some universities joined the FLA, USAS protested. Together with UNITE, the People of Faith Network and other groups, such as Hong Kong–based Labor Rights in China and the Honduran Women's Collective, then formed a Worker Rights Consortium (WRC). At least nine universities with-drew from FLA and provisionally joined WRC. The University of California and four other universities issued a report in Octo-ber 2000, specifying abusive and dangerous working conditions in United States and overseas factories that manufacture apparel with school logos. The report drew on a yearlong study to find that many universities adopted inadequate codes of conduct that are difficult to enforce.[22]

Actions by Coalitions

During the 2000 Democratic Convention in Los Angeles, a coalition of student, labor, immigrant, human rights, and faith-based groups (including the Mobilization for the Human Family, whose Sweatshop Action Committee I chair) marched through the garment district to the convention center in support of worker and immigrant rights. In particular, we were asking California governor Davis to enforce AB 633 (the antisweatshop legislation discussed above), President Clinton to support the Worker Rights Consortium, and Congress to repeal employer sanctions and grant an unconditional amnesty to immigrants.[23] "The workers' struggle has no borders" was an especially popular chant. Over two thousand people, mostly from Los Angeles, participated in the protest, including some garment workers who were speakers, monitors, and marchers. As we moved from 8th and Santee in the center of the garment district, others leaned out the windows of the buildings where they work, waving garments and flags in support.[24]

This coalition continues its efforts to resist injustice in apparel production, whether in Los Angeles or other parts of the world. Our most recent action was in solidarity with workers in Nicaragua resisting union busting. There were eight worker-supported, independent unions recognized by employers in Nicaragua in 1998, more than in all the other Central American countries combined. By 2000, only two were left. In the intervening year and a half, factory owners and managers in the Las Mercedes Free Trade Zone, outside of Managua, engaged in an extensive antiunion offensive. The National Labor Committee (U.S.) and the Campaign for Labor Rights, along with several other groups, organized an international solidarity campaign supporting workers in the two remaining unions—one at Mil Colores and the other at Chentex. Mil Colores, a small factory owned by Greg Miller, a U.S. citizen, rehired fired union members and continues to negotiate with the union. This is clearly a victory for the workers and the international solidarity campaign, especially if the factory continues to receive retailer contracts.[25]

Chentex, a much larger factory owned by Taiwanese consortium Nien Hsing, employs eighteen thousand Nicaraguan workers who produce twenty-five thousand pairs of jeans each day. Eighty percent of the workers are women, most of them age twenty-one or younger; 50 percent of them are single mothers. "In 1998, Chentex workers formed a union and signed an agreement with the management of the factory stating that a wage increase would be discussed the next year. The average pay for Chentex workers is $0.20 per pair of jeans, which are sold in the United States for an average price of $30.00." Zenayda Torres, a fired union official at Chentex, reported, "For the last five years, I worked as a sewing operator in the Chentex factory.... They fired me on May 26 of this year, along with all 11 union leaders and about 700 other women and men workers, all because we asked for an 8-cent wage increase." Taiwanese unions joined the international solidarity campaign demanding the rehiring of the workers and good-faith negotiations with the union. The campaign focused not just on Chentex and its manager, but also on the Nien Hsing consortium and the Taiwanese government, which had given funds to the consortium. In the spring of 2001, Nicaragua's highest court ordered that the fired workers be rehired. At first management refused, but on May 10 a historic agreement was signed by management and the union that provided for the rehiring of four union leaders and seventeen union members. Fired union leaders who were not rehired will work as union organizers.[26]

In October 2000, the U.S. government expressed its concern to the Nicaraguan government that the rights of workers under Nicaraguan law were not being enforced. Soon after, Charles Kernaghan, of the National Labor Committee, discovered that the U.S. military purchases large numbers of jeans from Chentex to sell in its PX stores.[27] This revelation makes the Corporate Code of Conduct proposed by Rep. McKinney all the more urgent.

Global Compact

UN secretary general Kofi Annan has taken leadership on the international front. At the January 1999 meeting of the World Economic Forum (the group of business leaders that meets yearly in Davos, Switzerland), he introduced a Global Compact that he hoped business would endorse. This compact draws on principles from the UN Declaration of Human Rights and the 1992 Earth Summit to articulate nine principles. The first two principles ask world business to support and respect international human rights. The next four ask world business to uphold freedom of association and the right to collective bargaining, the elimination of compulsory and forced labor, abolition of child labor, and prohibition of employment discrimination. The last three ask world business to take a precautionary approach to environmental challenges; promote greater environmental responsibility, and encourage the spread and development of environmentally friendly technologies.

In July 2000, some fifty multinational companies, including Dutch Shell and Nike, and twelve labor associations and watchdog groups signed the compact, which took eighteen months to negotiate. Annan cautioned companies that they risk eroding the consensus favoring free trade and investment if they do not respect human and environmental values. The pact binds the signers to a declaration of principles rather than a legal code of conduct. Because of this, several advocacy groups accused the United Nations of participating in a "bluewash," allowing some of the largest and richest corporations to wrap themselves in the United Nations' blue flag without requiring them to do anything new. Even so, some corporations did not want to sign. Since the collapse of world trade talks in Seattle in December of 1999 and ongoing street protests, others have been interested in forging alliances with some of their critics. The Global Compact is the most visible example of such alliances.[28] Given the lack of effective enforcement mechanisms, the Global Compact is little more than the U.S. Fair Labor Association on a global scale. Exploited workers and the environment deserve better.

As this overview makes clear, there are many possibilities to challenge "the thousands of oppressive realities" behind the food we eat and clothes we wear. In fact, it may seem that there are too many possibilities. While the "simple life" movement is an important option for individuals to consider, changing lifestyle alone will not sufficiently challenge the evils of global capitalism. Individuals should choose one or two issues of most concern to them, and then look for a group, organization, or movement that is addressing the issue. People of faith can begin by inquiring of the social justice agency of their denomination. The Internet can also lead to locating groups.

Also, there are various levels of involvement. The first might be researching an issue and then contributing financially to an organization addressing the issue. One can write letters, make phone calls, or visit store managers, corporate executives, and government representatives. This can be done by individuals, but likely will be more effective if done as part of a campaign. One might join a local group through the National Interfaith Committee for Worker Justice, where one develops personal relationships with local workers who are part of organizing or negotiating campaigns. Or one can engage in solidarity actions with workers in other parts of the world—part of one's imagined community. Here, one does not have direct relationships, but develops a sense of community through empathy and imagination by learning about people from reading, talks, or media programs. Many solidarity campaigns learned from the farmworkers, and bring workers from other countries to the United States to speak about conditions in their country. One can also participate in nonviolent demonstrations, which can be an effective way of presenting demands as well as raising public awareness, developing coalitions, and strengthening resolve.[29]

At times, we may feel that our efforts are making no real difference. I sometimes struggle with such feelings. Several things keep me going. One is to remember that even small differences count for the people affected by them. Another is to think about the Lilliput strategy mentioned at the beginning of this chapter. Thousands of groups around the globe are challenging the injustices of corporate-ruled globalization. Together, we can restrain the forces of injustice; we can create space for alternatives to develop. We need to remember how long it took to end slavery, or to gain the right for women to vote. We are just beginning to develop "people's globalization."

Questions for Discussion

1. What successful campaigns have you heard about or participated in? What do you consider the most important factors in a successful campaign?

2. Do you agree that unions are a most effective way of protecting workers' rights? Should U.S. labor law be changed to be more in line with international labor codes?

3. Does the idea of community-supported agriculture appeal to you? What would it take to make something like this happen in your community?

4. Are there ways other than the ones discussed in this chapter to make a difference in workers' lives?

Additional Resources

Behind the Label. www.BehindTheLabel.org. This site provides weekly updates, multimedia resources, and action alerts on sweatshops.

Cobb, John B., Jr., and Mobilization for the Human Family. "Responding to Sweatshops." Pp. 153–70 in *Speaking of Religion and Politics: The Progressive Church on Hot Topics.* Claremont, Calif.: Pinch Publications, 2000. The rationale for the Mobilization's antisweatshop work.

"Hot Peppers and Parking Lot Peaches: Evaluating Farmers' Markets in Low Income Communities." Community Food Security Coalition (CFSC), P.O. Box 209, Venice, CA 90294; Tel: 310-822-5410, Fax: 310-822-1440. Useful recommendations of voluntary and governmental actions to make high-quality food more accessible to low-income people.

Interfaith Center for Corporate Responsibility, 475 Riverside Drive, New York, NY 10115; Tel: 212-870-2295, Fax: 212-870-2023; www.domini.com/ICCR.html. An excellent resource for learning more about socially responsible investing and shareholder resolutions. Participated in successful effort to drop Wal-Mart from the Domini Socially Responsible Investing Index Fund in May of 2001 because of its refusal to open its subcontractors' plants to independent verification.

Paleczny, Barbara. *Clothed in Integrity: Weaving Just Cultural Relations and the Garment Industry.* Waterloo, Ont.: Wilfrid Laurier University Press, 2000. An interesting discussion of a Canadian antisweatshop campaign.

Sweatshop Watch. www.sweatshopwatch.org. A good starting point for activism on sweatshops, with several links to other organizations.

FIVE

Can We Really Make a Difference?

The greatest single threat to the global financial system is the absence of public support.

— Charlene Barshevsky,
U.S. Trade Representative, Clinton Administration, 1999

What is presented as an economic system governed by the iron laws of a kind of social nature . . . is in reality a *political system* which can only be set up with the active or passive complicity of the officially political powers. Against this political system, political struggle is possible.

— Pierre Bordieu, French sociologist and activist, 1998

We must look after our forests, our springs, our rivers and our wild animals; in fact all our natural resources. There is still time to fight for a new world, full of peace and harmony. Dear friends, we must not exchange the future of our children for a few coins. Let's be united, hand in hand with this new world that is for all of us.

— From a letter of the imprisoned environmentalist
peasant farmers of Mexico Rodolfo Montiel Flores
and Teodoro Cabrera García, 2000

In this final chapter the focus returns to the global dynamics and actors discussed in the first chapter. The devastating effects of neoliberalism documented there must be resisted and systemic transformation of the political economy advanced. Those of us who yearn for "a new world for all of us" must struggle together across borders of many kinds (race, gender, class, nation), a process called "people's globalization." Those who hold and benefit from concentrated political and economic power will not yield easily, but we have reasons to be hopeful. International movements of people committed to justice can make a difference.

100

I begin this chapter with a discussion of the debt forgiveness campaign of Jubilee 2000, noting its successes and limitations. I continue with an exploration of the emerging movement against corporate-ruled globalization and for people's globalization, evaluating its goals and strategies. I conclude with an ethic for just and sustainable community. This includes advocacy of human rights as a basis for establishing minimal levels of social justice, which we owe to each other as human beings and world citizens.

The various movements discussed in this chapter are vital instances of groups in "civil society" (as distinct from the nation-state and the economy) forming alliances to challenge the concentrated power of corporations and nondemocratic institutions such as the IMF, World Bank, and WTO in behalf of a common good. They include human rights, labor, women's, environmental, and religious groups. An important religious group in this regard is the World Council of Churches (WCC), a fellowship of 337 churches (denominations) in more than one hundred countries. This body is a truly global institution that some think is positioned to challenge concentrated political and economic power, particularly in alliance with other groups that share a vision of people's globalization.

Writing about the importance of these institutions in civil society, Benjamin R. Barber believes, "Sovereign nations remain the locus of democratic society and the only viable powers capable of opposing, subduing, and civilizing the anarchic forces of the global economy. International civil society, the emerging global alternative to world markets, needs the active support of sovereign states for its fragile new institutions to have even a modest impact." Within democratic countries, progressive groups can enhance "the voice of civil society" in the organization and governance of the world.[1]

Debt Forgiveness

Many of the world's poorest countries and their citizens suffer under a burden of unsustainable international debt. The WCC maintains, "Children and women are forced to bear the full costs of debt repayment through reductions in health, sanitation and clean water programs. In addition, by concentrating on exports, poor countries strip forests and overexploit land and non-renewable resources, further aggravating serious environmental problems. High levels of debt and economic degradation inevitably lead to social conflict and disintegration, in particular war." Most deeply indebted countries have not been able to resolve their debt problem. Although southern countries have paid their debt principal several times over, their debt has grown by 250 percent. "According to some estimates, from 1982 to 1998 indebted countries paid four times the original principal, yet at the same time their debt stocks went up by four times." This is because most poor countries experience trade deficits (only eleven of ninety-three low- and moderate-income countries currently have trade surpluses), which make it difficult to service their debt regularly. The service charges are then rolled over into new loans, dramatically increasing the outstanding debt.[2]

In 1996, the IMF and World Bank introduced an initiative to ease the debt burden of forty-one highly indebted poor countries (HIPCs). The debt of these countries, when concessionary terms are taken into account, totaled about $125 billion, nearly all owed to governmental agencies (others assess the total debt at closer to $216 billion). The goal of the HIPC initiative was to bring the debt down to a sustainable level (based on a debt-to-export ratio). Countries eligible for debt relief would have to establish a record of good policy performance, as defined by the IMF and World Bank. These policies included privatization, removing public subsidies from health and education, liberalization, and other reforms.[3] After three to six years, the country would reach a "decision point," when the IMF and World Bank would decide whether or not to reduce the country's principal and interest payments. After further compliance with these conditions, a country could arrive at a "completion point," at which time its debt principal would be reduced.

Jubilee 2000

About the same time as the HIPC initiative was introduced, faith-based activists launched a campaign of debt forgiveness called Jubilee 2000. They drew on biblical traditions of the Jubilee year, when slaves are set free and debts canceled (Leviticus 25, Isaiah 61, Luke 4; 2000 was a Jubilee year in the Roman Catholic calendar).

In recommendations adopted by the WCC, this biblical background was given:

> Through the sabbath-jubilee tradition, the Hebrew and Christian scriptures offer a critical mandate for periodically overcoming structural injustice and poverty and for restoring right relationships. In the earliest Hebrew sabbath traditions, consumption and exploitation of the land were limited by the sabbath and the sabbath year. People and animals were to rest every seventh day and the land every seventh year (Ex. 23:10–12). During the sabbath year, there was to be release from debts and slavery and during the jubilee year a restoration of all family lands (Lev. 25). These commandments are taken up in "the year of the Lord's favour" (Isa. 61:1–2a) and described in Isa. 65:17–25 as "new heavens and a new earth." In other words, justice brings peace for all God's creation. In the New Testament, Jesus extends the jubilee vision by proclaiming good news to the poor, release to the captives, sight to the blind and liberation of the oppressed. He taught his disciples to pray for the forgiveness of debts (as we forgive our debtors). Pentecost was characterized by the voluntary sharing of possessions, so that "there was not a needy person among them" (Acts 4:34, cf. Deut. 15:4).[4]

The WCC declared, "The jubilee is a recognition that, left to its normal and uninterrupted course, power becomes more and more concentrated in a few hands, that without intervention every society slides into injustice."[5] Jubilee 2000 called for a more generous and quicker write-off of external debts than the HIPC initiative offered. Its aim was to reduce poverty, not just make the debt more sustainable. It called upon leaders of the richest countries, the commercial banks, and other international financial institutions to write off, by the year 2000, the crushing international debts of impoverished countries burdened with a high level of human need and environmental distress. Debts were to be forgiven in a way that benefits ordinary citizens and facilitates their participation in determining public policy. Debt cancellation should also be done in ways that do not perpetuate or deepen poverty or environmental degradation. The process was to be transparent; a public commission, rather than the IMF and World Bank, would direct the process. The goal was to avoid recurring cycles of indebtedness, as had happened in the past.

The Jubilee 2000 campaign is an international one, with affiliates in sixty-nine countries. Over forty U.S. business organizations support the campaign. The movement uses mass mobilization, direct action, and Internet organizing to work toward its goals. The campaign has had some positive effect on the HIPC initiative. After Jubilee 2000 demonstrations at the 1998 G7 meeting in Cologne, the G7 governments (United States, United Kingdom, Canada, France, Germany, Italy, and Japan) agreed to write off $27 billion in debt to major creditors, which would have a leveraging effect that would result in about $100 billion in debt relief to poor countries. They also agreed to cut the period for countries to reach the "decision point" to three years. Finally, they adopted Jubilee 2000's commitment to poverty reduction, but required that HIPCs present plans for poverty reduction as a condition for debt relief.[6]

Jubilee 2000 kept the pressure on governments to follow through on these commitments. Jubilee 2000/USA actively lobbied Congress in support of legislation authorizing $435 million of the $920 million the United States had pledged at Cologne; it barely passed in October of 2000. This represents a tenfold increase in the debt relief line item in the foreign operations spending bill from two years before. (Congress also made a statement opposing user fees for education and health care imposed by the World Bank and IMF, acknowledging that they are harmful to impoverished communities.) Jubilee 2000/UK, a coalition that includes over ninety organizations, realized similar results.

Twenty-two countries reached the "decision point" at the end of 2000. Together, their principal and interest payments have been reduced by about 30 percent. Uganda is the only country to have reached the "completion point." Its debt principal ($2.3 billion) was reduced by 42 percent. This partial debt relief has brought some gain for Uganda. It was permitted to drop fees for school attendance (a usual condition for debt relief), which resulted in an 80 percent increase in enrollments. These improvements would not have been achieved as quickly without the pressure brought by Jubilee 2000. People working together can make a difference.

An Unresolved Issue

Although the debt crisis is being addressed, it has not been resolved. At the end of 2000, the total HIPC debt is $219 billion—$3 billion more than in 1996. Ann Pettifor, director of Jubilee 2000/UK, states, "The bulk of the unpayable debts are still in place. We have yet to achieve real justice for a billion people." Jubilee South challenged the movement to push for more effective and meaningful debt relief. Their concerns are reflected in the current goals of Jubilee 2000/USA, which demands that creditor governments and international financial institutions "immediately suspend debt service payments and the accrual of interest on loans from heavily indebted poor countries." They point out that "further accrual of interest merely makes it more expensive for the debts to be removed from the books while continued payments further harm the indebted countries."[7]

The conditions attached to both the loans and debt relief continue to place an enormous burden on poor people. In looking at the impact of World Bank loans, World Bank economist William Easterly found that "a lot of the countries that have gotten a lot of lending from the IMF and World Bank are worse off." In contrast, he found that countries such as India and China were better at poverty reduction during periods of economic expansion than countries under IMF control.[8]

Jubilee 2000 asserts that current World Bank and IMF reform programs increase poverty, inequality, and environmental degradation. They condemn these destructive policies and call for "the establishment of some more neutral and open arbitration process, whereby nations can appeal for relief, and the terms and conditions of such arrangements are given open and due consideration." The campaign also wants to add substantial debt relief for heavily indebted middle-income countries. They challenge existing initiatives that do not appropriately address "odious" or illegitimate debts that are patently unjust in nature.[9] The WCC points to military and corrupt dictatorships and those of the apartheid regime as having incurred the most unacceptable kind of debt, defined in international law as odious debts.

Jubilee 2000/USA is deeply troubled by the Poverty Reduction

Strategy Paper (PRSP) process, issued by the World Bank and IMF in response to criticism about their failure to reduce poverty. "From the start the campaign questions the legitimacy of the IMF taking the role of judging countries in terms of poverty reduction, an area in which the IMF has no expertise." In many countries, citizen participation in the process was quite limited. Most disturbing is "the injustice that macro-economic reform conditions have not been subordinated to poverty reduction concerns or made subject to transparent, democratic and participatory decision-making."[10] Activist Shalmali Guttal calls the PRSP little more than hurriedly worked-over versions of standard World Bank-IMF policy papers" that are not likely to make a dent in poverty, given the failure of earlier policies.[11]

The Dakar Declaration, issued by Jubilee South in the fall of 2000, is more uncompromising in its demands. It calls for the end of conditions for countries to participate in the HIPC process, no structural adjustment program for new loans, and immediate cancellation of illegitimate debts. It also calls for governments in the south to publicly investigate and audit the debt, suspend payments until investigations have been made, and withhold payment of illegitimate debts. The movement is planning for national people's tribunals on debt and structural adjustment programs, like the one held in Brazil in September of 2000. This was organized and supported by a coalition of religion, labor, and other groups, in which the results of a plebiscite were announced. The Dakar Declaration asks northern groups to increase the pressure on international financial institutions and governments for debt cancellation, and to move toward the abolition of the IMF, World Bank, and WTO.[12] This links the campaign for debt forgiveness to the anticorporate globalization movement. Some in this group are also considering asking for reparations from northern countries for the centuries of exploitation carried out through enslavement and colonization.

Movement for a People-Centered Globalization

Kevin Danaher of Global Exchange, a human rights group that has taken leadership in the campaign against corporate globalization, compares globalization from above with a bottom-up form. Globalization from above is controlled by wealthy elites and driven by a hunger for more wealth and power—greed. In contrast, bottom-up globalization focuses on meeting human need. John Powell and S. P. Udayakumar, writing in the journal *Poverty and Race*, describe the changes wrought by globalization:

> People are now brought together as consumers but kept apart as citizens. The transformed role of government is not to protect citizens or the precious safety net of public space but to protect and facilitate the flow of capital. So today we speak of free markets but not of free labor. We speak of an expanding global market, but a diminishing public space, and we hardly speak at all of citizen participation and justice.

They conclude that this is an "authoritarian vision" in which "armies police nations and people, so capital might be free." The police response to nonviolent protestors during the 1999 WTO meeting in Seattle fits this description.[13]

The WCC offers an alternative vision, one rooted in the struggles of African people for liberation from colonialism. This vision lives on "in the struggles of the people for daily livelihood, to sustain their community life, to be nourished by the rich traditions and values inherited from the past, to live in harmony with the earth, to find space to express themselves." People long "to live in dignity in just and sustainable communities." They note that people from all parts of the world resonate with this vision, because we experience the same yearnings.[14]

Limiting Corporate Power

The movement against globalization from above has had some victories in limiting the expansion of corporate power. A coalition of human rights, labor, religious, and other groups, including the Third World Network, the Council of Canadians, and the International Forum on Globalization, has been successful in delaying the Multilateral Agreement on Investments (MAI). This agreement was negotiated by the Organization for Economic Cooperation and Development (OECD), and intended to restrict the power of any of its twenty-nine member countries and other signatories to regulate foreign investment. In reality, this means that investors' rights take precedence over any member country's social or environmental policies, and that investors have the right to sue countries for "lost" profits. In the fall of 1998, OECD withdrew MAI in the face of opposition from activists in over ten countries who leaked the draft to the public. The *Toronto Globe and Mail* wrote that the high-powered OECD politicians were "no match for a global band of grassroots organizations, which, with little more than computers and access to the Internet, helped derail the deal."[15] A broader coalition stopped a new round of negotiations by the WTO meeting in Seattle, which likely would have included an agreement similar to MAI.

A crucial struggle beginning in the spring of 2001 is working to stop the Free Trade Area of the Americas (FTAA), which would be an extension of NAFTA to all the Americas, and to keep the U.S. Congress from giving fast-track authority to President Bush. Granting this authority would permit him to negotiate this treaty in a way that would prohibit any Congressional amendments, a clearly undemocratic approach. A current focus of the movement is a "right to know" legislative proposal that would require U.S. transnationals to collect and disclose crucial data on workplace conditions and environmental damage in their overseas production, including that of subcontractors and suppliers.[16]

Groups protesting globalization from above are not just objecting to proposals that would expand corporate-ruled globalization; they are also developing their own proposals. In one such proposal, Jeremy Brecher, Tim Costello, and Brendan Smith have developed a draft of an "Alternative Program for the Global Economy," whose aim is "to provide a win-win framework for the many constituencies converging into globalization from below." This program attempts to bring these groups interests, needs, and concerns into a complementary relationship, rather than a contradictory one. There are seven key elements to this alternative program:

1. "Level labor, environmental, social, and human rights conditions upward." The first step is to improve conditions for those caught in the race to the bottom. The ultimate goal is to in-

corporate minimum labor, social, environmental, and human rights standards into national and international law. The authors think that the first step would lead to an expansion of employment and markets, which would "generate a virtuous circle of economic growth."

2. "Democratize institutions at every level from local to global." The point here is to make institutions accountable to those they affect.

3. "Make decisions as close as possible to those they affect." The goal is "a multilevel global economy." Initiative and power are to be concentrated at as low a level as possible, with higher-level regulation established where necessary. This is articulation of the principle of subsidiarity, prominent in Roman Catholic social teaching.

4. "Equalize global wealth and power." The economic advancement of the most oppressed and exploited people, "including women, immigrants, racial and ethnic minorities, and indigenous peoples," should be a policy priority with the aim of increasing their power, capability, resources, and income.

5. "Convert the global economy to environmental sustainability." This requires that the current process of globalization be stopped and replaced with a focus on meeting human needs in ways that reduce the negative impact of the economy on the environment.

6. "Create prosperity by meeting human and environmental needs." A crucial goal is to "to create a new kind of full employment" based on satisfying these needs. The authors hope that this would lessen the need for the millions of rural people who are forced to migrate in search of work.

7. "Protect against global boom and bust." Neoliberal policies that insist on freedom of capital must be replaced with capital controls that aim to increase economic security for ordinary people.[17]

Rep. Bernie Sanders (I-Vt.) has introduced the Global Sustainable Development Resolution to the U.S. Congress (H.R. 479), which resonates with many of the principles in Brecher, Costello, and Smith's proposal. It would set up U.S. and UN Commissions on the Global Economy to investigate the effect of globalization on workers, industry, and the environment. It also includes provisions for shrinking the World Bank and IMF, as well as a tax on financial speculation. Although it is very unlikely that this resolution will be passed in the near future, it does provide a basis for progressive advocacy.[18]

There is growing support for some form of capital control. One such proposal is called the Tobin Tax, after economist James Tobin, who developed its details. Several cities around the world, as well as the Canadian Parliament, have endorsed resolutions in support of a Tobin Tax. In the summer of 2000, over three hundred economists from forty-two countries issued a statement in support. They noted that properly functioning financial markets might play a positive role in providing funds for socially beneficial projects, which can be liquidated by the investor if needed. But highly speculative financial markets may be exceedingly damaging to a society, as we saw in chapter 1. Financial markets can be destabilized, with impacts spreading across the society. The ability of governments to use effective countermeasures is diminished by expansion of these markets. Taxes on speculative financial activity make speculation more costly, reducing the volume of speculation. This contributes to stabler financial markets. "The historical record of financial transactions taxes, as well as long-standing evidence on the success of other forms of financial regulation, indicates that taxes on financial speculation can be successfully implemented." The Tobin Tax proposal includes provisions for using the proceeds to meet crucial social needs.[19]

Advancement of the Oppressed

There is also growing support for making the economic advancement of the most oppressed and exploited people a policy priority, as suggested in the fourth plank of the "Alternative Program for the Global Economy." Since the success of the Grameen Bank in Bangladesh in making small loans to poor women who used them to build income-generating projects that substantially improved their families' well-being, "micro-credit" programs like these are viewed by some as *the* solution to poverty. Grameen Bank founder Muhammad Yunus cautions that experience shows that unless *the poorest of the poor* are specifically targeted by these programs, "they will be excluded as they are from almost every other opportunity." He further cautions that micro-credit alone will not empower the poor or lead to any significant drop in absolute poverty; other programs, like girls' education and youth employment opportunities, are also necessary.[20]

As noted above, the alternative program for the global economy aims to find complementary rather than contradictory relationships between the goals, interests, and needs of the various groups in the people's globalization movement. Widespread support for a Tobin Tax and for making the advancement of the poor a policy priority seems to indicate that the proposal accomplishes this aim. Are there, though, crucial debates that the proposals attempt to smooth over? Two important issues that need more exploration, in my judgment, are the status of the IMF, World Bank, and WTO, and the issue of limits to economic growth.

Reforming Economic Institutions and Concepts

In the discussion of the Jubilee 2000 movement, I noted the debate over whether the IMF and the World Bank should be reformed or replaced. There is a similar debate about the WTO. Clearly, several of the points in the "Alternative Program for the Global Economy," if enacted, would dramatically reform institutions like these. However, a clarification of which types of reforms are useful and which are not is needed. An editorial in the *Multinational Monitor* just prior to the WTO's December 1999 meeting in Seattle provides this. The editorial called for the dismantling of the WTO, due to three fatal flaws. First, the WTO's trade rules purposefully prioritize trade and commercial considerations above all other values. Second, the WTO deliberately takes precedence over countries' decisions about how their own economies should be structured and corporations regulated. Third, the WTO does not just regulate global trade, but actively promotes it. The editorial realizes that citizen movements may not yet be powerful enough to shut down the WTO. It cautions, though, that "reforms that add new areas of competence to the WTO or enhance its authority go in the wrong direction." This includes areas that may seem desirable, such as labor rights. On the other hand, "reforms that limit the WTO's authority," such as limiting application of its agricultural rules in the south, "are necessary and beneficial in their own right." These cautions are also appropriate in regard to any proposed reforms of the IMF and the World Bank.[21]

Walden Bello proposes radical reduction of the power of the WTO to make it simply another international institution coexisting with and being checked by other international organizations, like the United Nations Commission on Trade and Development (UNCTAD); agreements, including multilateral environmental ones; and regional groupings, like the evolving trade blocs in southern regions.[22]

The need for economic growth is another area of debate that the "Alternative Program" seems not to fully address. As written, the proposal seems to support what is called "sustainable development." In its own recommendations on globalization, the WCC charges that this concept "does not question the underlying paradigm of continuous and unlimited progress and growth." A WCC study raised concerns about unlimited growth: because of the world's limited resources, permanent economic growth threatens ecological sustainability; its products are unevenly distributed; it increases inequality, with the rich minority "wasting a great volume of the earth's resources and living far above the level of human need."[23] Is the proposed alternative program's "virtuous" growth really different from unlimited growth?

The sustainable-development approach is similar to what is called the Human Development Consensus, advocated by the UNDP and UNICEF. This approach advocates what it calls "pro poor growth," which focuses on policies that are labor intensive and employment generating, and also encourage equity. It is one alternative to the Washington Consensus, a name for current neoliberal IMF and U.S. Treasury policies discussed in chapter 1. Another alternative is the "People-Centered" consensus, which is led by various citizen alliances. A primary difference between these two alternatives is that the Human Development consensus believes in economic growth through free markets.[24]

Another important issue is not addressed by the "Alternative Program" at all: what counts as economic activity? Current definitions limit economic activity, a basic factor in calculating gross national product (GNP) and economic growth, to market exchange or paid work. In her landmark 1984 book, *Counting for Nothing,* Marilyn Waring demonstrated that current GNP statistics include things that are bad for human health and the environment, such as carcinogenic chemicals in foods, pollution from factories, and preparation for nuclear war. Yet, the subsistence farming and unpaid domestic work that contribute significantly to human well-being are not counted. Much of this unpaid work is done by the world's women and is essential to their families' well-being. We saw in chapter 1 that this workload has increased with IMF structural adjustment policies. Yet, since it is not included in GNP, not only is its importance unrecognized, but also the negative impact on women's health of this increased burden will likely go unaddressed by public policy.[25]

Economist Lourdes Beneria recently wrote of a continuing "resistance to the measuring of work and production of goods and services that sustain and enhance human well-being," although there is sophisticated methodological and theoretical work on how this activity can be included. In 1996, the Independent Commission for Population and Quality of Life called for a redefinition of work "in a broad sense that encompasses both employment and unpaid activities." The Commission believes that this will benefit "society as a whole, families as well as individuals," and will help ensure more equitable distribution of the wealth generated. A fully adequate alternative economic program would include a redefinition of economic activity. As Beneria claims, the questions underlying this issue are "what is value and what is of value to society."[26]

An Ethic for Just and Sustainable Community

As has been evident throughout this book, contrasting ethical visions are at the heart of the debate about globalization. Rapidly increasing inequalities between nations and within nations, and threats to ecological and economic sustainability, are central ethical issues. The Jubilee 2000 movement cautions that economic, social, and environmental problems in some countries threaten the well-being of people everywhere. In today's world, none of us can prosper for long unless all of us have the things we need for lives of sufficiency and dignity.

Neoliberals believe that the solution to these inequalities is integration into the global economy, with openness to global capital and global competition. They are willing to accept what they see as "natural" inequalities created by capitalist globalization, rather than sacrifice the loss of freedom and economic efficiency that is involved when various governmental agencies intervene to remedy these inequalities. Neoliberals tend to downplay threats to ecological sustainability and trust in technological "fixes" to environmental problems that arise. Their position is challenged on both empirical and ethical grounds.[27]

The WCC challenges this logic of globalization with "an alternative way of life of community in diversity." This is grounded in a life-centered vision that affirms God's gift of life to all creation. Four essentials for this vision need to be nurtured: (1) *participation*, the optimal inclusion of all involved at every level; (2) *equity*, basic fairness that extends to all life forms; (3) *accountability*, "the structuring of responsibility towards one another and Earth itself"; (4) *sufficiency*, a commitment to meet the basic needs of all life possible and to develop "a quality of life that includes bread for all but is more than bread alone." In this life-centered vision, basic human needs, individual and community rights, and environmental protection take precedence over debt repayment or economic efficiency. All the world's religions seem to share the belief that one is responsible for meeting another's needs.[28]

Economic Rights

Basic needs claims can be translated into economic rights. Article 25 of the 1948 UN Declaration of Human Rights states, "Everyone has the right to a standard of living adequate for the health and well-being of self and family, including food, clothing, housing, medical care and necessary social services." These are part of what is called the second generation of human rights, which includes economic, social, and cultural rights. Political and civil rights make up the first generation of human rights. First-generation rights are understood as negative rights; the freedom of individuals is not to be unjustly interfered with. Second-generation rights are seen as positive rights; they presume a community that takes responsibility for the satisfaction of everyone's basic needs.[29]

Although powerful rhetorically, the UN Declaration of Human Rights has no binding authority. There are two covenants that implement these rights: the International Covenant on Civil and Political Rights and the International Covenant on Economic, Social, and Cultural Rights. Both covenants had to be ratified by thirty-six nations before they became legally binding on those nations; this happened in 1976. The United States ratified the first covenant in 1992, but is unlikely to ratify the second without a major shift in its thinking about rights. Ecologically minded readers might charge that this focus on human rights is anthropocentric, even if we include the right to a safe environment among the second-generation rights. David Korten addresses the relationship between the environment and basic needs when he develops criteria for the use of the earth's resources: "The appropriate concern is whether the available planetary resources are being used in ways that (1) meet the basic needs of all people, (2) maintain biodiversity, and (3) assure the sustained availability of comparable resource flows to future generations."[30] Korten notes that our present economic system fails to meet any of these three criteria. Ethicist Timothy Gorringe suggests, "If the standard of living enjoyed by the North cannot be generalized, then the issue of consumption has to be addressed by the wealthy nations."[31]

The international human rights movement, including the groups that concentrate on women's human rights, has focused primarily on civil and political rights. This focus does not speak adequately to the concerns of many of the world's women. Barbara Stark finds that of the two generations of rights, it is the second generation as articulated in the International Covenant on Economic, Social, and Cultural Rights that may well make the most difference for women.[32] These second-generation rights are distinct from the "right to development," adopted by the UN General Assembly in 1986. The development model underlying this document, according to Corinne Kumar-D'Souza, "has brought with it the dispossession of the majority of the people, the desacralizing of nature, the destruction of the way of life of entire cultures, and the degradation of women."[33]

Robust national and international movements for social and economic rights are crucial in this time of corporate globalization, with its emphasis on expanding trade rights, intellectual property rights, and investor rights. The challenge is to develop a normative vision and notion of community on which to base collective action for the realization of economic and social rights. The decent society is one such vision. Avishai Margalit defines a decent society as "one whose institutions do not humiliate its members." Dehumanization is a primary form of humiliation. The World Bank defines absolute poverty as "a condition of life so characterized by malnutrition, illiteracy and disease as to be beneath any reasonable definition of human decency." Decency is thus an institutional agenda grounded in universal responsibility.[34]

Certainly, the notion of a decent society is a useful basis for realizing economic and social rights. So too is the notion of justice, especially if we move beyond liberal notions of procedural justice. Ethicist Beverly Harrison claims that a biblical sense of justice "focuses on concrete human need and is therefore substantive." We are required by our sense of justice to engage existing inequities and to critically analyze and protest against "institutional arrangements that pervasively perpetuate and deepen social inequities.[35] This sense is grounded in recognition of our common human dignity and a commitment to the common good.

We have learned from our experience with civil and political rights that legislation is only a first step. Persons need to be informed of their rights, and effective enforcement mechanisms established. I know of two quite different but equally effective approaches to informing people of their rights. One is the Los Angeles Garment Workers Center program to distribute booklets to workers (in their own languages), which include a summary of their newly won right to back wages from manufacturers and retailers, logs to record their hours, and information on how to make claims if their rights have been violated. The second is the use of street theater by an organization of Ugandan women lawyers to inform women of their newly gained rights to protection from domestic violence and to inheritance. They also provide free and low-cost mediation and legal services. The challenge is to extend programs like this into rural areas.[36]

A successful conclusion to the seven-year-old human rights struggle led by the indigenous people from the state of Chiapas in Mexico (popularly called the Zapatistas) seemed possible in 2001 when newly elected President Vicente Fox supported constitutional reform legislation that would recognize the economic and cultural rights of Mexico's indigenous peoples. At the January 1, 1994, launch of the North American Free Trade Agreement (NAFTA), the Zapatista National Liberation Army (EZLN) rose up against free trade and neoliberalism. (They were also protesting the loss of their communal land rights, which came about through a change in the Mexican Constitution as a precondition for Mexico's entry into NAFTA.) The Zapatista movement has made savvy use of the Internet to inform the world of its positions. "Instead of humanity neoliberalism offers us stock market value indexes, instead of dignity it offers us globalization of misery, instead of hope it offers us emptiness, instead of life it offers us . . . terror."[37] The movement stayed strong despite military repression and at least one massacre, buoyed in part by an international solidarity movement (see chapter 3).

Although the government has reneged on implementing a 1996 agreement on indigenous rights and culture (the San Andreas Accords), its central provisions were included in the proposed legislation. However, the legislation that passed the Mexican Congress in April of 2001 seriously compromised these provisions and was rejected by the Zapatistas as well as nongovernmental groups like the Fray Bartolomé de las Casas Human Rights Center. Its critics charge it is a "counter-reform" because it excludes specific elaborations "of indigenous rights in regard to autonomy" and the right of indigenous peoples "to collective use and enjoyment of the natural resources found on their lands and territories." The law's supporters believe that it represents an advance in recognition of indigenous rights and culture since, when ratified, it brings the Mexican constitution in line with international conventions on indigenous rights. The legislation also includes provisions to ensure respect for the rights of indigenous women and girls. As of this writing, the legislation has just been ratified by a sufficient num-

ber of states for constitutional reform to be enacted.[38] Even though
the Zapatistas and their supporters did not accomplish their objec-
tives at this point, they were effective in raising awareness of crucial
prerequisites for building just and sustainable communities.

The Need for Solidarity

Building just and sustainable communities around the world will
continue to demand solidarity from those of us who are committed
to a new world that is for all of us. Effective solidarity requires participation in communities that nurture dialogue across difference,
critical consciousness and compassion, and practices of resistance
and accountability. Solidarity also requires heart. I like to call the
ethic that I have attempted to develop in this book an "ethic of
heart." When I think of people practicing solidarity, I think of
people with hearts that are tender, warm, caring, passionate, strong,
brave; of people who hearten each other in the face of heartbreak-
ing realities; of many hearts beating in rhythm with the heart of
the universe. "Heart" is a good symbol for some of the distinctive
contributions that feminist ethics brings to an ethic for just and sustainable community: emotion, relationality, and care. Stout hearts,
clear eyes, open ears, dirty hands—all are essential for our common
task.[39]

In this chapter, we have seen that there are movements that are
challenging the dehumanizing logic of neoliberalism. There have
been some significant successes: improving the HIPC debt-relief program, and stopping both the Multilateral Agreement on Investments
and a new round of WTO negotiations. The movement is developing its own vision and program for a people-centered globalization.
The elements of an ethic for just and sustainable community are
becoming clear.

Even so, the task before us is daunting. In spite of our best efforts so far, the debt of poor countries increases, as does the gap
between the world's wealthy and poor, with unbearable human and
ecological costs. At the same time, more and more people are join-
ing together to say "No!" to a dehumanizing form of globalization
and to build a world of just, sustainable communities. "Let us learn
to find joy in the struggle," Muneer Ahmed, a young attorney and
activist, challenged us at the opening of the Los Angeles Garment

Workers Center. May we indeed find joy in our many struggles for a world with enough for all.

Questions for Discussion

1. Do you agree with the goals of the Jubilee 2000 campaign? What, if anything, is missing from its program?

2. Discuss each of the seven planks of the "Alternative Program for the Global Economy." What are the strengths and weaknesses of this program?

3. Discuss the WCC's four essentials for an alternative way of life of community in diversity. Do you see other essentials? What is your vision of the common good?

4. Discuss the differences between first- and second-generation rights? Do you agree that we need economic, social, and cultural rights to establish just, sustainable community?

5. What comes to your mind when you hear the term "ethic of heart"? How else might one characterize an ethic like the one developed in this book?

Additional Resources

Boff, Leonardo, and Virgil Elizondo, eds. *Ecology and Poverty: Cry of the Earth, Cry of the Poor.* Maryknoll, N.Y.: Orbis Books, 1995. A useful discussion of the connections between poverty and ecology.

Catholic Voices on Beijing: A Call for Social Justice for Women. Washington, D.C.: Catholics for a Free Choice, 2000. A critical Catholic feminist discussion of Catholic social teaching.

de Gaay Fortman, Bastiaan, and Berma Klein Goldewijk. *God and the Goods: Global Economy in a Civilizational Perspective.* Geneva: World Council of Churches, 1998. A fruitful collaboration between one of the commissioners of the WCC Program Unit on Justice, Peace, and Creation (Fortman) and a member of the Roman Catholic Justice and Peace Commission (Goldewijk).

Ringe, Sharon H. *Jesus, Liberation, and the Biblical Jubilee: Images for Ethics and Christology.* Philadelphia: Fortress Press, 1985. A scholarly discussion of the Jubilee tradition.

Schroyer, Trent, ed. *A World That Works: Building Blocks for a Just and Sustainable Society.* New York: Bootstrap Press, 1997. A useful discus-

sion of truly alternative economies from The Other Economic Summit
(TOES).

Who's Counting? Marilyn Waring on Sex, Lies and Global Economics.
National Film Board of Canada, 1995. www.nfb.ca. An educational
and entertaining video on global economics.

Your Story Is Our Story: The Ecumenical Decade and Beyond. Video high-
lights of 1998 Ecumenical Decade of the Churches in Solidarity with
Women Conference, including an excerpt of the keynote address by
Dr. Musimbi Kanyoro. Available from the WCC, at www.wcc-coe.org.

Notes

Preface

1. I am grateful to Genevieve Beeton for bringing this ad to my attention when she was a student in my feminism and economics class at Immaculate Heart College Center.

2. See Jerry H. Gill, *Borderlinks: The Road Is Made by Walking* (Tucson: Borderlinks, 1999), or www.borderlinks.org.

3. David Held and Anthony McGrew, eds., *The Global Transformations Reader: An Introduction to the Globalization Debate* (Cambridge: Polity Press, 2000), 3–4.

4. Thomas Friedman, *The Lexus and the Olive Tree: Understanding Globalization* (New York: Farrar, Strauss and Giroux, 1999), 287, 209. I find a certain irony in Friedman's use of the Saudi prince, given his country's record on democracy and human rights.

5. Thomas Frank, *The Nation*, October 30, 2000, 18. See also Thomas Frank, *One Market under God: Extreme Capitalism, Market Populism, and the End of Economic Democracy* (New York: Doubleday, 2000), 15, 56–57. This book is a must-read.

6. Pamela K. Brubaker, *Women Don't Count: The Challenge of Women's Poverty to Christian Ethics* (Atlanta: Scholars Press, 1994), now available from Oxford University Press.

7. My interest in drawing from daily life is informed by the work of Dorothy Smith, especially *The Everyday World as Problematic: A Feminist Sociology* (Boston: Northeastern University Press, 1987).

Chapter 1: Just What Is Globalization Anyway?

1. Nicholas D. Kristof, "World Ills Are Obvious, the Cures Much Less So," *New York Times*, February 18, 1999.

2. Ulrich Beck, "What Is Globalization?" in Held and McGrew, eds., *Global Transformations Reader*, 100–102. When I was in Uganda, I saw the other side of cultural globalization—some would say cultural imperialism. Television was dominated by CNN, Pat Robertson's 700 Club, and U.S. cop shows.

3. Mark Weisbrot, *Globalization: A Primer* (Washington, D.C.: Center for Economic and Policy Research, 1999). www.cepr.net/GlobalPrimer.htm.

4. Sarah Anderson and John Cavanagh, with Thea Lee and the Institute for Policy Studies, *Field Guide to the Global Economy* (New York: New Press, 2000), 5.

5. Rob van Drimmelen, *Faith in a Global Economy: A Primer for Christians* (Geneva: World Council of Churches, 1998), 7.

6. Thomas L. Friedman, *The Lexus and the Olive Tree: Understanding Globalization* (New York: Farrar, Strauss and Giroux, 1999), 357.

7. Peter Marcuse, "The Language of Globalization," *Monthly Review* 52, no. 3 (July–August 2000), accessed at http://monthlyreview.org. I am grateful to Russell Stockard for bringing this article to my attention.

8. Van Drimmelen, *Faith in a Global Economy*, 8.

9. E. K. Hunt and Howard J. Sherman, *Economics: An Introduction to Traditional and Radical Views*, 4th ed. (New York: Harper and Row, 1981), 21.

10. Carol Johnston, *The Wealth or Health of Nations: Transforming Capitalism from Within* (Cleveland: Pilgrim Press, 1998), 31.

11. Beverly Wildung Harrison, "The Older Person's Worth in the Eyes of Society," in *Making the Connections: Essays in Feminist Social Ethics*, ed. Carol Robb (Boston, Beacon Press, 1985), 291 n. 10.

12. Anderson and Cavanagh, *Field Guide*, 12–13.

13. The data on illegal trade is from ibid., 14; on armaments trade from *New Internationalist* (December 2000): 18.

14. Peter Dicken, "A New Geo-economy," in Held and McGrew, eds., *Global Transformations Reader*, 252–55.

15. Anderson and Cavanagh, *Field Guide*, 66.

16. Van Drimmelen, *Faith in a Global Economy*, 22–23.

17. Ibid., 38, 41–43.

18. Anderson and Cavanagh, *Field Guide*, 66–67.

19. Van Drimmelen, *Faith in a Global Economy*, 18.

20. Anderson and Cavanagh, *Field Guide*, 68.

21. Ibid., 17.

22. Susan George, "A Short History of Neo-Liberalism," Conference on Economic Sovereignty in a Globalizing World, March 24–26, 1999, available at www.globalexchange.org.

23. Van Drimmelen, *Faith in a Global Economy*, 38.

24. Nicholas D. Kristof, with Edward Wyatt, "Who Sank, or Swam, in Choppy Currents of a World Cash Ocean," *New York Times*, February 15, 1999.

25. Anderson and Cavanagh, *Field Guide*, 67

26. Ibid, 18; van Drimmelen, *Faith in a Global Economy*, 9; Ankie Hoogvelt, "Globalization and the Postcolonial World," in Held and McGrew, eds., *Global Transformations Reader*, 356.

27. "The Reality of Aid 2000," available at www.realityofaid.org; Virginia Hammell, "Summary of the FY1999 Budget for Foreign Aid/USAID and Exchanges/USIA," available at www.nasulgc.org.

28. Nicholas D. Kristof, with David E. Sanger, "How U.S. Wooed Asia to Let Cash Flow In," *New York Times*, February 16, 1999.

29. David C. Korten, "Sustainability and the Global Economy," in *Visions of a New Earth: Religious Perspectives on Population, Consumption, and Ecology*, ed. Howard Coward and Daniel C. Maguire (Albany: State

University of New York Press, 2000), 40. In this discussion of financial speculation I am also drawing on William Greider, *One World, Ready or Not: The Manic Logic of Global Capitalism* (New York: Simon and Schuster, 1997), 227–58; David C. Korten, *When Corporations Rule the World* (West Hartford, Conn.: Kumarian Press, 1994), 185–226; and Kevin Danaher, "Globalization and the Downsizing of the American Dream," available at www.globalexchange.org.

30. Cited in Timothy Gorringe, *Fair Shares: Ethics and the Global Economy* (New York: Thames and Hudson, 1999), 86.

31. David Held and Anthony McGrew, "The Great Globalization Debate: An Introduction," in idem, eds., *Global Transformations Reader,* 2, 5, 7, 38. Held and McGrew identify two contrasting groups: globalists and skeptics. Beverly W. Harrison identifies at least four different theories of economic globalization: neoliberal and developmental, two distinct theories that both rely on neoclassical economics; alternative economics; and postcolonial theories (from a presentation in the Religion and Social Science Section of the American Academy of Religion, November 2000). I also benefited from conversations with Rebecca Todd Peters on this topic.

32. Cited in Korten, "Sustainability," 29. My account of Bretton Woods institutions is also informed by Greider and van Drimmelen.

33. Van Drimmelen, *Faith in a Global Economy,* 39.

34. Lori Wallach and Michelle Sforza, *Whose Trade Organization? Corporate Globalization and the Erosion of Democracy* (Washington, D.C.: Public Citizen, 1999), 115–18.

35. Van Drimmelen, *Faith in a Global Economy,* 53.

36. My discussion of neoliberalism draws on George, "Short History of Neo-Liberalism."

37. Walden Bello, *Dark Victory: The United States, Structural Adjustment, and Global Poverty* (London: Pluto Press, 1994), 19. The Heritage Foundation was also influential in dismantling elements of the U.S. safety net, such as so-called welfare reform.

38. Shalmali Guttal, "Women and Globalisation: Some Key Issues," presentation at the conference Strategies of the Thai Women's Movement in the Twenty-First Century, Bangkok, March 28–29, 2000; see www.focusweb.org. On the three types of consensus, see John B. Cobb Jr., ed., and Mobilization for the Human Family, "The Globalization of Economic Life," in *Speaking of Religion and Politics: The Progressive Church on Hot Topics* (Claremont, Calif.: Pinch Publications, 2000), 171–88.

39. Friedman, *The Lexus and the Olive Tree,* 86–87.

40. Joseph Stiglitz, "The Insider," *The New Republic* 222, nos. 16–17 (April 17–24, 2000): 56–60.

41. Rosi Braidotti, Ewa Charkiewics, Sabine Hausler, and Saskia Wieringa, *Women, the Environment and Sustainable Development: Towards a Theoretical Synthesis* (London: Zed Books with INSTRAW, 1994), 17–18.

42. Altha Cravey, *Women and Work in Mexico's Maquiladoras* (Lanham, Md.: Rowman and Littlefield, 1998), 6.

43. Ibid., 15, 21, 11. Cravey points to Article 806.30 and 807.00 of the

Tariff Schedule of the United States, which "significantly reduced the costs to transnational corporations of manufacturing outside the United States by charging duty only on the value added (usually labor costs) of goods assembled elsewhere."

44. *Miami Herald*, August 11, 2000.

45. Greider, *One World, Ready or Not*, 270.

46. Korten, "Sustainability," 30.

47. Mark Weisbrot, *Globalization: A Primer* (Washington, D.C.: Center for Economic and Policy Research, 1999). www.cepr.net/GlobalPrimer.htm.

48. George, "Short History of Neo-Liberalism."

49. All statistics, except for advertising, are from the 1998 UNDP *Human Development Report*. Advertising data is from "Economics Forever: Building Sustainability into Economic Policy," Panos Media Briefing No. 38, March 2000, cited in "Sustainability: The Facts," *New Internationalist* (November 2000): 19.

50. Guttal, "Women and Globalization."

51. Anderson and Cavanagh, *Field Guide*, 44–46.

52. George, "Short History of Neo-Liberalism." For the Bolivian story, see "The Fight for Water and Democracy: An Interview with Oscar Olivera," *Multinational Monitor* (June 2000): 15–19. The movement was successful in overturning the law privatizing water.

53. Robert Scott, Thea Lee, and John Schmitt, "Trading Away Good Jobs: An Examination of Employment and Wages in the U.S., 1979–94," Economic Policy Institute, 1997. "Working Hard, Earning Less: The Story of Job Growth in America," National Priorities Project, 1989. See also Danaher, "American Dream."

54. Joel Millman, "The Outlook," *Wall Street Journal*, March 8, 1999; SourceMex, February 23, 2000, March 8, 2000, available at ladb.unm.edu/sourcemex.

55. Bello, *Dark Victory*, 7–8.

56. My discussion of recolonization draws on M. Jacqui Alexander and Chandra Talpade Mohanty, who assert that "global realignments of capital have simply led to further consolidation and exacerbation of capitalist relations of domination and exploitation" (*Feminist Genealogies, Colonial Legacies, Democratic Futures* [New York: Routledge, 1997], xvii). Their claim is characteristic of postcolonial theories of globalization. Data on commodities is from Anderson and Cavanagh, *Field Guide*, 10–11.

57. Wallach and Sforza, *Whose Trade Organization?* 110–11.

58. Saskia Sassen, "Women's Burden: Counter-Geographies of Globalization and the Feminization of Survival," *Journal of International Affairs* 53, no. 2 (spring 2000): 503–24, accessed through Proquest online database. My discussion of the debt crisis also draws on van Drimmelen, *Faith in a Global Economy*; Gorringe, *Fair Shares*; and Cobb, ed., "Should Debt Be Forgiven?" in *Religion and Politics*, 189–205.

59. Cited in Gorringe, *Fair Shares*, 66.

60. Sassen, "Women's Burden," and information from the Jubilee 2000/USA website, www.j2000usa.org/j2000.

61. Greider, *One World, Ready or Not,* 236–37. Statistics on the cost of bailout are from Kristof and Wyatt, "World Cash Ocean."

62. Anderson and Cavanagh, *Field Guide,* 46. For an updated list of cases brought under this provision of NAFTA, see Mary Bottar, "NAFTA's Investor 'Rights,' A Corporate Dream, A Citizen Nightmare," *Multinational Monitor* (April 2001): 9–13.

63. Weisbrot, *Globalization.* See also Carlos Heredia Zubieta, "The Mexican Economy: Six Years into NAFTA," www.developmentgap.org.

64. Held and McGrew, *Global Transformations,* 339.

65. Guttal, "Women and Globalisation," n. 35.

66. My discussion in this paragraph draws on Guttal, "Women and Globalisation," Sassen, "Women's Burden," and these articles: Margaret Kalaiselvi, "Economic Globalization and Its Impact on Women," in *Envisioning a New Heaven and a New Earth,* ed. Lalrinawmi Raltz et al. (Delhi: NCCI/SPCK, 1998), 113–17; M. Patricia Connelly, "Gender Matters: Global Restructuring and Adjustment," *Social Politics* 3, no. 1 (spring 1996): 12–31.

67. Connelly, "Gender Matters," 13.

68. Nancy Forsythe, Roberto Patricio Korzeniewicz, and Valerie Durrant, "Gender Inequalities and Economic Growth: A Longitudinal Evaluation," *Economic Development and Cultural Change* 48, no. 3 (April 2000): 573–617.

69. Saskia Sassen, *Globalization and Its Discontents: Essays on the New Mobility of People and Money* (New York: New Press, 1998), 41. Statistics are from Anderson and Cavanagh, *Field Guide,* 24.

70. Sassen, "Women's Burden," accessed through Proquest online database.

71. Sassen, *Globalization,* 15, 29. Statistics on border patrol are from Anderson and Cavanagh, *Field Guide,* 34.

72. George, "Short History of Neo-Liberalism."

Chapter 2: What Does Globalization Have to Do with Daily Life?

1. World Bank, press release on *World Development Report 2000/2001: Attacking Poverty,* September 2000.

2. "Twelve Myths about Hunger," *Institute for Food and Development Policy Backgrounder* 5, no. 3 (summer 1998), www.foodfirst.org, based on Frances Moore Lappé, Joseph Collins, and Peter Rosset, with Luis Esparza *World Hunger: Twelve Myths,* 2nd ed. (New York: Grove Press, 1998).

3. Lisa Smith and Lawrence Haddad, *Explaining Child Malnutrition in Developing Countries: A Cross-Country Analysis* (Washington, D.C.: International Food Policy Research Institute, 2000), Research Report 111, available at www.ifpri.org.

4. "Twelve Myths" (italics added). The Zairean farmer's quotation is from Lisa McGowan, "Bailouts for Bankers, Burdens for Women," available at www.50years.org/factsheets/bailouts.html.

5. Harriet Friedman, "Remaking 'Traditions': How We Eat, What We Eat and the Changing Political Economy of Food," in *Women Working the NAFTA Food Chain: Women, Food and Globalization*, ed. Deborah Barndt (Toronto: Second Story Press, 1999), 48.

6. Figures on corn are from the U.S. Department of Agriculture, on rice from the National Federation of Rice Producers; from SourceMex, January 19, 2000, available at ladb.unm.edu/sourcemex.

7. Ibid.

8. Deborah Barndt, "Whose 'Choice'? 'Flexible' Women Workers in the Tomato Food Chain," in idem, ed., *Women Working*, 66.

9. Cited in ibid., 63.

10. Ibid, 63, 69, 71.

11. Egla Martinez-Salazar, "The 'Poisoning' of Indigeneous Migrant Women Workers and Children: From Deadly Colonialism to Toxic Globalization," in Barndt, ed., *Women Working*, 100.

12. Antoineta Barron, "Mexican Workers on the Move: Migrant Workers in Mexico and Canada," in Barndt, ed., *Women Working*, 122.

13. Martinez-Salazar, "Migrant Women Workers and Children," 102–3.

14. Friedman, "Remaking 'Traditions,' " 40–41.

15. John Hubner, "Farm Workers Face Hard Times: Middlemen Maximize Profits by Paying as Little as Possible," *San Jose Mercury News*, July 8, 2000.

16. See Fran Ansley, "Putting the Pieces Together: Tennessee Women Find the Global Economy in Their Own Backyards" in Barndt, ed., *Women Working*, 142–60. For a discussion of this fire and its relation to the interstructuring of the class exploitation, racism, and sexism that underlie this event, see Mary Hobgood, *Dismantling Privilege: An Ethics of Accountability* (Cleveland: Pilgrim Press, 2000).

17. Alan Howard, "Labor, History, and Sweatshops in the New Global Economy," in *No Sweat: Fashion, Free Trade, and the Rights of Garment Workers*, ed. Andrew Ross (New York: Verso, 1997), 151–72.

18. Julie Su, "El Monte Thai Garment Workers: Slave Sweatshops," in Ross, ed., *No Sweat*, 143–49. This incident happened less than a year after I moved to southern California and prompted my involvement in the antisweatshop movement. A few of these young women went on to become activists. I will tell that story in chapter 4.

19. Christopher Scheer, " 'Illegals' Made Slaves to Fashion," *The Nation*, September 11, 1995, 238.

20. *Sweatshop Watch* 6, no. 3 (fall 2000): 3; at www.sweatshopwatch.org.

21. Ibid.

22. Ibid., 1–2.

23. Lance Compa, *Unfair Advantage: Workers' Freedom of Association in the United States under International Human Rights Standards* (New York: Human Rights Watch, 2000), 7.

24. Edna Bonacich and Richard Appelbaum, *Behind the Label: Inequality in the Los Angeles Apparel Industry* (Berkeley: University of California Press, 2000), 71, 55.

25. Gloria Anzaldúa, *Borderlands: La Frontera* (San Francisco: Aunt Lute Books, 1987), 3.

26. Bonacich and Appelbaum, *Behind the Label,* 67.

27. Altha Cravey, *Women and Work in Mexico's Maquiladoras* (Lanham, Md.: Rowman and Littlefield, 1998), 11, 74.

28. Interpress Service, February 28, 2000.

29. William Greider, *One World, Ready or Not: The Manic Logic of Global Capitalism* (New York: Simon and Schuster, 1997), 337–39.

30. Annette Bernhardt, "The Wal-Mart Trap," *Dollars and Cents* (September–October 2000): 23–24.

31. Charles Kernaghan, *Made in China: The Role of U.S. Companies in Denying Human and Worker Rights* (New York: National Labor Committee, 2000).

32. Dexter Roberts and Aaron Bernstein, "A Life of Fines and Beating," *Business Week* (October 2, 2000): 122–28.

33. Bernhardt, "The Wal-Mart Trap," 24–25. In April 1999, a Texas judge fined Wal-Mart $18 million after the corporation was found guilty of withholding evidence from the courts fifteen times in a single year (*New Internationalist* [July 2000]: 29).

34. Pierre Bordieu, *Acts of Resistance: Against the Tyranny of the Market* (New York: Free Press, 1998), 85.

35. Cravey, *Women and Work,* 18, 24, 111–25.

36. Patricia Fernandez-Kelly, "Reading the Signs: The Economics of Gender Twenty-five Years Later," *Signs* 25, no. 4 (summer 2000): 1109–10.

37. Ibid., 1110.

Chapter 3: What Does Faith Have to Do with Globalization?

1. Quoted in L. M. Sixel, "The Two Sides of Flap over Saipan Labor," *Houston Chronicle,* July 30, 1999.

2. Barbara Rumscheidt, *No Room for Grace: Pastoral Theology and Dehumanization in the Global Economy* (Grand Rapids: Eerdmans, 1998).

3. Among the theologians and ethicists who have made this claim is James M. Childs Jr., *Greed: Economics and Ethics in Conflict* (Minneapolis: Fortress Press, 2000), esp. 73–76. We must remember that in actuality there is no one Christian church, but many different denominations. In chapter 5, I will discuss efforts of the World Council of Churches to address globalization.

4. H. Richard Niebuhr, *Christ and Culture* (New York: Harper and Row, 1951). Besides accommodation, Niebuhr identified four other postures: Christ above culture, Christ and culture in paradox, Christ transforming culture, and Christ against culture. Some contemporary theologians believe that we need to replace this typology, as it assumes that we can know Christ apart from culture. Mary McClintock Fulkerson offers another approach: "To replace the dualities of Christian identity versus culture and Christian culture versus secular culture I propose that theological social criticism think of Christian participation in the imagined worlds that produce subjects in various locations. That way culture's determination by the economic and

political can be marked" ("Toward a Materialist Christian Social Criticism: Accommodation and Culture Reconsidered," in *Changing Conversations: Religious Reflection and Cultural Analysis*, ed. Dwight N. Hopkins and Sheila Greeve Davaney [New York and London: Routledge, 1996], 53). This essay was helpful in shaping my approach to this chapter.

5. Fulkerson, "Materialist Christian Social Criticism," 53.

6. Garth Kasimu Baker-Fletcher, *Dirty Hands: Christian Ethics in a Morally Ambiguous World* (Minneapolis: Fortress Press, 2000), 59. Baker-Fletcher is drawing on the work of sociologist Pierre Bordieu.

7. Roger Gottlieb, *A Spirituality of Resistance: Finding a Peaceful Heart and Protecting the Earth* (New York: Crossroad, 1999), 75, 90, 64.

8. Pamela K. Brubaker, "Sisterhood, Solidarity and Feminist Ethics, *Journal of Feminist Studies in Religion* (spring–fall 1993): 53–66.

9. Gottlieb, *Spirituality of Resistance*, 46, 50.

10. Rumscheidt, *No Room for Grace*, 74.

11. Pierre Bordieu, *Acts of Resistance: Against the Tyranny of the Market* (New York: Free Press, 1998), 43.

12. For an insightful discussion of this topic, see Ronald F. Thiemann, *Religion in Public Life: A Dilemma for Democracy* (Washington, D.C.: Georgetown University Press, 1996).

13. Robert Benne, "Lutheran Ethics," in *The Promise of Lutheran Ethics*, ed. Karen L. Bloomquist and John R. Stumme (Minneapolis: Fortress Press, 1998), 20.

14. Ibid., 21.

15. This literature is voluminous. See, for example, *The Dictionary of Feminist Theology*, ed. Shannon Clarkson and Letty Russell (Louisville: Westminster John Knox Press, 1996).

16. A reading that seems to resonate with Benne's identifies holiness, particularly sexual purity, as the core moral vision of Christianity. With the current debate on homosexuality, this seems to be the dominant interpretation of the core vision, at least in the United States. Heterosexual marriage is privileged, homosexuality condemned. This reading is often supported by reference to the Levitical "Holiness Code," as well as the letters of Paul. Cultural anthropologist Mary Douglass interprets this as a purity code, which creates binary oppositions between pure and impure, clean and unclean. In my judgment, it can lead to self-righteousness and demonization of the other. Some interpreters think that Jesus challenged this code—for instance, his healing of the bleeding woman. He did not condemn her for touching him when she was bleeding, even though in doing this she had violated the Holiness Code. Rather, he told her that her faith had healed her. For further discussion, see Pamela Brubaker, "A Terror of Touch: Homosexuality Debates and Changing Churches," *Journal of Theology and Sexuality* (March 1997): 56–70.

17. Wolfgang Stegemann, *The Gospel and the Poor*, trans. Dietlinde Elliott (Philadelphia: Fortress Press, 1984), 64. Stegemann's position is characteristic of liberation theology. In comparison, Benne contends that the direction of the Lutheran ethical tradition for public policy is that of

"Christian realism." Ulrich Duchow, also a German Lutheran, takes a position similar to Stegemann's in *Global Economy, A Confessional Issue for the Churches?* (Geneva: World Council of Churches, 1987).

18. Fulkerson, "Materialist Christian Social Criticism," 52–53

19. Gottlieb, *Spirituality of Resistance,* 165, 30.

20. Ibid., 70, 97.

21. Ibid., 97–98.

22. Ibid., 159, 161.

23. Rumscheidt, *No Room for Grace,* 101.

24. Ibid., 132.

25. Fulkerson, "Materialist Christian Social Criticism," 55–56.

26. I am grateful to Ada María Isasi-Díaz for introducing me to the term "kin-dom," which I prefer to "kingdom." My understanding of solidarity has been deepened by her work. See chapter 5, "Solidarity: Love of Neighbor in the Twenty-First Century," in her *Mujerista Theology* (Maryknoll, N.Y.: Orbis Books, 1996).

27. Susan Brooks Thistlethwaite and Peter Crafts Hodgson, "The Church, Classism and Ecclesial Community," in *Reconstructing Christian Theology,* ed. Rebecca Chopp and Mark Lewis Taylor (Minneapolis: Fortress Press, 1994), 307. *Basileia* is the Greek word for "kingdom" in the New Testament.

28. I am offering *one* interpretation of these parables. I agree with those who claim that scripture—and literature—has multiple meanings. However, that does not mean that any interpretation is as good as another. A good interpretation attends both to the historical context of the text and to the sociocultural context of the interpreter. For a useful and accessible interpretive approach, see Ched Myers et al., *Say to This Mountain: Mark's Story of Discipleship* (Maryknoll, N.Y.: Orbis Books, 1996).

29. My reading is indebted to Marcus Borg, *Meeting Jesus Again for the First Time: The Historical Jesus and the Heart of Contemporary Faith* (San Francisco: Harper, 1994). I find his portraits of Jesus compelling, but I have come to question the claim that these are accurate representations of the "historical Jesus." I follow Kwok Pui-lan's recent critique of the current quest for the historical Jesus (presented at the 1999 meeting of the American Academy of Religion in Boston). She persuasively argues that, as with the first quest, the Jesus who is found in the later ones bears an uncanny resemblance to those who are searching. She offers other images for Jesus—such as corn or rice—from two-thirds world Christians. These images help keep us aware of the difference that sociocultural context makes and also of the centrality of embodied human need in doing theology.

30. Bruce V. Malchow, "Social Justice in the Wisdom Literature," *Biblical Theology Bulletin* 12 (1982): 122–23.

31. Sondra Ely Wheeler, *Wealth as Peril and Obligation: The New Testament on Possessions* (Grand Rapids: Eerdmans, 1995), 144. She adds that the general obligations can be assessed only in light of actual material conditions "in concrete and situated communities." Wheeler provides an excellent list of questions drawn from biblical teaching for congregations to use in making such judgments (pp. 138–43). Some interpreters argue

that the issue is not wealth, but greed. For an insightful ethical analysis, see James Childs, *Greed: Economics and Ethics in Conflict* (Minneapolis: Fortress Press, 2000).

32. Mary E. Hobgood, *Dismantling Privilege: An Ethics of Accountability* (Cleveland: Pilgrim Press, 2000), 34. This is also an epistemological conversion from assumptions of a neutral or objective knowing.

33. For example, Dermot Cox claims that the fundamental requirement of righteousness "is simply a matter of 'clean hands and a pure heart'," which "is effectively a re-interpretation of the tora of Lev. 19:2: 'you must be holy, for I, the Lord your God, am holy' " ("Peace and Peacemakers in the 'Writings' of the Old Testament," *Studia Missionalia* 38 [1989]: 7). I do think, though, that we can strive for a "pure heart." I would interpret this as the honesty to recognize our complicity—even though involuntary—in unjust systems and structures (cf. note 16, p. 128).

34. My understanding of imagined communities has been informed by the work of Chandra Talpade Mohanty, both in the coauthored introduction to *Third World Women and the Politics of Feminism*, ed. Chandra Talpade Mohanty, Ann Russo, and Lourdes Torres (Bloomington: Indiana University Press, 1991), and her article, "Under Western Eyes: Feminist Scholarship and Colonial Discourses," in that same volume.

35. The cross, and the doctrine of substitutionary atonement in particular, have been important topics of debate in feminist theological scholarship, which is beyond the scope of this chapter. Two useful reviews of the debate, with original contributions, are Elisabeth Schüssler Fiorenza, "The Execution of Jesus and the Theology of the Cross," in *Jesus: Miriam's Child, Sophia's Prophet* (New York: Continuum, 1994), 97–128, and JoAnne Terrell, *Power in the Blood? The Cross in the African American Experience* (Maryknoll, N.Y.: Orbis Books, 1998). I also find Karen Baker-Fletcher's discussion helpful: "The Strength of My Life," in *Embracing the Spirit: Womanist Perspectives on Hope, Salvation and Transformation*, ed. Emilie Townes (Maryknoll, N.Y.: Orbis Books, 1997), 122–30.

36. Mary Solberg, *Compelling Knowledge: A Feminist Proposal for an Epistemology of the Cross* (Albany: State University of New York Press, 1997), 133.

37. Ibid., 151.

38. My paraphase is inspired by Solberg's discussion of Luther in *Compelling Knowledge*, 70, 83–84, and by David Loy, "The Religion of the Market," in *Visions of a New Earth: Religious Perspectives on Population, Consumption, and Ecology*, ed. Howard Coward and Daniel C. Maguire (Albany: State University of New York Press, 2000), 15–28. I am grateful to Lara Medina for helping me see more clearly the connection I am making between these two theologies.

39. Terrell, *Power in the Blood?* 112.

40. Emilie Townes, "Living in the New Jerusalem: The Rhetoric and Movement of Liberation in the House of Evil," in *A Troubling in My Soul: Womanist Perspectives on Evil and Suffering*, ed. Emilie Townes (Maryknoll, N.Y.: Orbis Books, 1993), 84.

41. Ibid.

42. Schüssler Fiorenza, *Jesus,* 126. In the chapter from which this quotation is taken, she contrasts the empty tomb tradition, in which women are the primary actors, with the appearance tradition, which serves to authorize male authority.

43. Beverly W. Harrison, "The Power of Anger in the Work of Love," in *Making the Connections: Essays in Feminist Social Ethics,* ed. Carol Robb (Boston: Beacon Press, 1985), 19.

44. Alexander Cockburn and Ken Serverstein, "The Demands of Capital," *Harper's* (May 1995): 66.

45. Harrison, "Power of Anger," 9–10.

46. Townes, "New Jerusalem," 89. The Evangelical Lutheran Church in America's social statement "Sufficient, Sustainable Livelihood for All" is available online at www.elca.org. For a discussion of a variety of denominational statements on economic life, see van den Berg, *God and the Economy.* The rendering of Jesus' proclamation is from Ivone Gebara, *Longing for Running Water: Ecofeminism and Liberation* (Minneapolis: Fortress Press, 1999), 84.

47. Elsa Tamez, "When the Horizons Close upon Themselves: A Reflection on the Utopian Reason of Qohelet," in *Liberation Theologies, Postmodernity, and the Americas,* ed. David Batsone et al. (New York: Routledge, 1997), 66.

Chapter 4: What Can I Do?

1. Jeremy Brecher and Tim Costello, *Global Village or Global Pillage: Economic Restructuring from the Bottom Up* (Boston: South End Press, 1994).

2. Saskia Sassen, *Globalization and Its Discontents: Essays on the New Mobility of People and Money* (New York: New Press, 1998), xxiv, xxxvi.

3. See Paul More et al., *The Other Los Angeles: The Working Poor in the City of the Twenty-First Century* (Los Angeles: Los Angeles Alliance for a New Economy, 2000).

4. John Hubner, "Farm Workers Face Hard Times," *San Jose Mercury News,* July 8, 2000.

5. This history is drawn from "The Rise of the UFW," available at www.ufw.org; and "La Causa," from the United Farm Workers archives at Wayne State University, available at www.ruether.wayne.edu/thecause.html.

6. James Rainey, "Farm Workers Union Ends 16-Year Boycott of Grapes" *Los Angeles Times,* November 22, 2000.

7. Margaret Reeves et al., "Fields of Poison: California Farmworkers and Pesticides," Pesticide Action Network North America, 2000; see www.panna.org/panna/resources/documents/fieldsAvail.dv.html. Workers in Arizona fare no better. The mission statement of Arizona's Department of Agriculture is "to regulate and support Arizona agriculture in a manner that encourages farming, ranching, and agribusiness while protecting consumers and natural resources." Note that it makes no mention of protecting agricultural workers.

8. Human Rights Watch, "Fingers to the Bone: United States Failure to Protect Child Farmworkers," June 2000, available at www.hrw.org.

9. Ibid. I make a similar argument on behalf of children and their families in "Making Women and Children Matter: A Feminist Theological Ethic Confronts Welfare Policy," in *Welfare Policy: Feminist Critiques,* ed. Elizabeth Bounds, Pamela Brubaker, and Mary Hobgood (Cleveland: Pilgrim Press, 1999), 25–46.

10. Human Rights Watch, "Fingers to the Bone." I am thinking, for instance, of the successful lawsuit against Microsoft by its contract employees to be recognized as regular employees eligible for benefits. The Bordieu term is from *Acts of Resistance: Against the Tyranny of the Market* (New York: Free Press, 1998), 85.

11. Daniel Imhoff, "Community Supported Agriculture," in *The Case against the Global Economy and for a Turn toward the Local,* ed. Jerry Mander and Edward Goldsmith (San Francisco: Sierra Club Books, 1996), 425.

12. Ibid., 426, 428.

13. Ibid., 433.

14. Debbie Field, "Putting Food First: Women's Role in Creating a Grassroots Food System Outside the Marketplace," in *Women Working the NAFTA Food Chain: Women, Food and Globalization,* ed. Deborah Barndt (Toronto: Second Story Press, 1999), 193–208.

15. George White and Patrick McDonnell, "Sweatshop Workers to Get $2 Million," *Los Angeles Times,* October 24, 1997.

16. For background information and updates on the situation in Saipan, as well as the lawsuits, see *Sweatshop Watch* 4, no. 1 (spring 1998); 5, no. 1 (spring–summer 1999); 5, no. 2 (fall 1999); 6, no. 2 (summer 2000); available at www.sweatshopwatch.org.

17. CoopAmerica provides up-to-date information on boycotts as well as responsible retailers at www.coopamerica.org. Kitty Krupat, "From War Zone to Free Trade Zone: A History of the National Labor Committee," in *No Sweat: Fashion, Free Trade, and the Rights of Garment Workers,* ed. Andrew Ross (New York: Verso, 1997), 51–77.

18. *Garment Workers and the Struggle for Justice* (Los Angeles: Asian Pacific American Legal Center, n.d.), 7.

19. *Sweatshop Watch* 5, no. 2 (fall 1999) 7, no. 2 (summer 2001).

20. Russell Mokhiber and Robert Weissman, "Big Ideas on Corporate Accountability and Global Sustainability," June 2000, a "Focus on the Corporation Column" posted at www.corporatepredators.org. Mokhiber and Weissman are coauthors of *Corporate Predators: The Hunt for MegaProfits and the Attack on Democracy* (Monroe, Maine: Common Courage Press, 1999).

21. Richard Appelbaum and Peter Dreier, "The Campus Anti-sweatshop Movement," *The American Prospect* (September–October 1999): 71–78. For model procurement policies, see www.uniteunion.org/sweatshops/cities/cities.html.

22. *Sweatshop Watch* 4, no. 3 (December 1998), and Teofilo Reyes, "Stu-

dents Win Big," *Labor Notes* (April 2000): 5, 11; also Tanya Schevitz, "Study Says Campus Suppliers Abuse Foreign Workforce," *San Francisco Chronicle*, October 7, 2000. The "Independent Initiative Study" is available at www.ucop.edu/ucophome/coordrev/policy/initiative-report.pdf. Massachusetts Institute of Technology professor Dara O'Rourke's critique of the study is available at web.mit.edu/dorourke/www. The United Students Against Sweatshops website is at www.usasnet.org; Worker Rights Consortium at www.workersrights.org.

23. See chapter 2 for discussion of the connection between worker and immigrant rights.

24. The best coverage of this march was William Booth and Rene Sanchez, "2,000 Rally in Streets against Sweatshops in Front of a Billboard of Franklin Roosevelt and Martin Luther King," *Washington Post*, August 18, 2000.

25. "Victory at Mil Colores," *Campaign for Labor Rights Alert,* posted on November 28, 2000. Alerts are available at the Campaign for Labor Rights website, www.summersault.com/~agj/clr.

26. Daisy Pitkin, "Background on the Chentex Campaign," *Campaign for Labor Rights Alert*, posted on December 8, 2000; also David Gonzalez, "Nicaragua's Trade Zone: Battleground for Unions," *New York Times*, September 16, 2000; Campaign for Labor Rights Update, April 2001.

27. Doris Hajewski, "U.S. Targets Kohl's Suppliers; Concerns Raised about Worker Rights," *Milwaukee Journal Sentinel*, October 13, 2000; Associated Press, "Sweatshop Makes Jeans Sold on U.S. Bases, Suit Says," *Los Angeles Times*, December 6, 2000. This incident brings to mind the military equipment produced in maquiladoras along the U.S.-Mexican border.

28. Joseph Kahn, "Multinationals Sign U.N. Pact on Rights and Environment," *New York Times*, July 27, 2000. The Global Compact and the names of its signers are available at www.unglobalcompact.org. For an in-depth critique, see Kenny Bruno, "Perilous Partnerships: The UN's Corporate Outreach Program," *Multinational Monitor* (March 2000): 24–26.

29. The National Interfaith Committee for Worker Justice, based in Chicago, has a network of local interfaith groups in over twenty-five states. Call 773-728-8400, e-mail nicwj@igc.org, or see www.igc.org/nicwj.

Chapter 5: Can We Really Make a Difference?

1. Benjamin R. Barber, "Globalizing Democracy," *The American Prospect* 11, no. 20 (September 11, 2000), www.prospect.org/archivesv11-20/barber-b.html. This is a useful, if somewhat idealistic, discussion of the role of civil society in relation to the nation-state and the market.

2. World Council of Churches, *Together on the Way,* report from the Eighth Assembly, Harare, Zimbabwe, December 1998, at www.wcc-coe.org. Estimates on debt increase from "Women's Burden: Counter-Geographies of Globalization and the Feminization of Survival," *Journal of International Affairs* 53, no. 2 (spring 2000), accessed through Proquest online database. Explanation is from Ellen Frank, "Disarming the Debt Trap," *Dollars and Sense* (March–April 2001), 10. Trade deficits would not create such problems for indebted countries if they were not required to repay their debts in

U.S. dollars. In addition to the WCC and Sassen, my discussion draws on John B. Cobb Jr., ed., and Mobilization for the Human Family, "Should Debt Be Forgiven?" in *Speaking of Religion and Politics: The Progressive Church on Hot Topics* (Claremont, Calif.: Pinch Publications, 2000), 189–205; and resources from the Jubilee 2000 campaign, available at www.j2000usa.org, www.jubilee2000uk.org, and www.jubileesouth.net.

3. See chapter 1 for a discussion of these conditions.

4. World Council of Churches, *Together on the Way*, section 5.2, "The Debt Issue: A Jubilee Call to End the Stranglehold of Debt on Impoverished Peoples."

5. Ibid., section 8.4, "Policy Reference Committee II Report, Appendix II: Globalization."

6. In addition to the resources already mentioned, this section draws on Marie Michael, "Jubilee 2000: Drop the Debt, Not the Campaign," *Dollars and Sense* (March–April 2001): 11–12. For a list of the countries included in the debt reduction program and the extent of relief for each country, see www.jubilee2000uk.org/media/endyear211200.html.

7. Pettifor cited in Michael, "Jubilee 2000," 12. "Jubilee 2000 USA End of the Year Statement 2000," www.j2000usa.org/updates/endyear.html.

8. Cited in Michael, "Jubilee 2000," 12.

9. "End of the Year Statement 2000."

10. Ibid.

11. Shalmali Guttal, "The End of Imagination: The World Bank, the International Monetary Fund and Poverty Reduction," at www.focusweb.org.

12. For the Dakar Declaration, see www.jubileesouth.net. See also the Uganda Debt Network, www.udn.or.ug.

13. Kevin Danaher, "Seven Arguments for Reforming the World Economy," www.globalexchange.org; John Powell and S. P. Udayakumar, "Race, Poverty and Globalization," *Poverty and Race* (May–June 2000), at www .globalexchange.org/economy/econ101/globalization072000.htm.

14. World Council of Churches, *Together on the Way*, section 8.4, "Policy Reference Committee II Report, Appendix II: Globalization."

15. Cited in Sarah Anderson and John Cavanagh, with Thea Lee and the Institute for Policy Studies, *Field Guide to the Global Economy* (New York: New Press, 2000), 95. For more information on MAI, see www.tradewatch .org. For an analysis of the impact of the Seattle movement, see William Greider, "Trading with the Enemy," *The Nation* (March 26, 2001): 11–14. For a list of successful, targeted Internet campaigns, such as protection of vulnerable forests from logging in various countries, see Global Response, an international letter-writing network of environmental activists in partnership with indigenous, environmentalist, and peace and justice organizations around the world, at www.globalresponse.org.

16. For more on fast track and FTAA, see www.tradewatch.org. In 1997 and 1998, Congress refused to give President Clinton fast-track authority.

17. Jeremy Brecher, Tim Costello, and Brendan Smith, *Globalization from Below: The Power of Solidarity* (Cambridge, Mass.: South End Press, 2000). The authors have a useful website at www.villageorpillage.org.

18. The resolution is available at www.netprogress.org.

19. For more information on the Tobin Tax, see the website of the Center for Economic and Policy Research (Washington), one of the founders of the Tobin Network USA, at www.cepr.net. At its 1998 assembly, the WCC endorsed the Tobin Tax as part of "initiatives for a new financial system."

20. Ismail Serageldin and Muhammad Yunus, "Empowerment Will Always Trump Charity," *Los Angeles Times,* June 30, 2000.

21. "Dismantle the WTO," *Multinational Monitor* (October–November 1999), 5, available at www.essential.org/monitor/monitor.html. It is important to be clear that the *Multinational Monitor* does not oppose labor rights; it opposes giving the WTO power over labor rights.

22. Walden Bello, "Why Reform of the WTO Is the Wrong Agenda," available at www.focusweb.org. The *Multinational Monitor* also has editorials calling for the shutdown of the IMF (May 2000) and the World Bank (June 2000). Ellen Frank (see note 2, p. 133) has a useful proposal for a central bank to replace the IMF and the World Bank.

23. World Council of Churches, *Together on the Way,* "Adopted Recommendations," no. 20; Julio de Santa Ana, *Sustainability and Globalization* (Geneva: WCC Publications, 1998), 10.

24. I am drawing on the discussion in John B. Cobb Jr., ed., and Mobilization for the Human Family, "The Globalization of Economic Life," in *Speaking of Religion and Politics: The Progressive Church on Hot Topics* (Claremont, Calif.: Pinch Publications, 2000), 171–88. There is also a range of views within the Washington Consensus. Thomas Friedman accepts their neoliberal program but recognizes the need for some form of "social safety net," if for no other reason than to keep those excluded from globalization's benefits from rising up against it (*The Lexus and the Olive Tree: Understanding Globalization* [New York: Farrar, Strauss and Giroux, 1999], 364–66).

25. Waring traces the way that GNP accounting methods were first developed by John Maynard Keynes to pay for World War II. These methods were then adopted by the United Nations for international use. Waring's book was published in the United States as *If Women Counted: A New Feminist Economics* (San Francisco: Harper and Row, 1988).

26. Lourdes Beneria, "The Enduring Debate over Unpaid Labour," *International Labour Review* 138, no. 3 (1999): 287–309. For a discussion of UN efforts in this regard, see chapter 5, "Work," in the United Nations, *The World's Women, 2000: Trends and Statistics,* 3rd ed. (New York: The United Nations, 2000).

27. This discussion of neoliberalism draws on David Held and Anthony McGrew, eds., *The Global Transformations Reader: An Introduction to the Globalization Debate* (Cambridge: Polity Press, 2000), 28. The first two chapters of my book document the empirical grounds for claiming that neoliberalism has failed. See also "Scorecard on Globalization 1980–2000" (Washington, D.C.: Center for Economic and Policy Research, 2001) available at www.cepr.net.

28. World Council of Churches, *Together on the Way,* "Recommenda-

tions on Globalization," no. 23. Data on world religions is from Bastiaan de Gaay Fortman and Berma Klein Goldewijk, *God and the Goods: Global Economy in a Civilizational Perspective* (Geneva: World Council of Churches, 1998), 60.

29. My discussion draws on Fortman and Goldewijk, *God and the Goods,* and Darryl M. Trimieux, *God Bless the Child That's Got Its Own: The Economic Rights Debate* (Atlanta: Scholars Press, 1997).

30. David Korten, "Sustainability and the Global Economy," in *Visions of a New Earth: Religious Perspectives on Population, Consumption, and Ecology,* ed. Howard Coward and Daniel C. Maguire (Albany: State University of New York Press, 2000), 33.

31. Timothy Gorringe, *Fair Shares: Ethics and the Global Economy* (New York: Thames and Hudson, 1999), 75.

32. Cited in Saskia Sassen, "Toward a Feminist Analytics of the Global Economy," in *Globalization and Its Discontents: Essays on the New Mobility of People and Money* (New York: New Press, 1998), 96. See also Rebecca J. Cook, ed. *Human Rights of Women: National and International Perspectives* (Philadelphia: University of Pennsylvania Press, 1994).

33. Corinne Kumar-D'Souza, "The Universality of Human Rights Discourse," in *Women, Violence and Nonviolent Change,* ed. Aruna Gnanadason, Musimbi Kanyoro, and Lucia Ann McSpadde (Geneva: World Council of Churches, 1996), 32.

34. Avishai Margalit and the World Bank are cited in Fortman and Goldewijk, *God and the Goods,* 60–61.

35. Beverly W. Harrison, "The Politics of Energy Policy," in *Making the Connections: Essays in Feminist Social Ethics,* ed. Carol Robb (Boston: Beacon Press, 1985), 177. See also the eloquent call of the U.S. Conference of Catholic Bishops for a new American experiment in economic rights, in *Economic Justice for All: Catholic Social Teaching and the U.S. Economy* (Washington, D.C.: United States Catholic Conference, 1986). Fortman and Goldewijk (*God and the Goods,* 59) question whether justice can be an adequate grounding for human rights, because of criticisms of John Rawls's liberal theory of rights. They do not consider a theory of justice connected to need, like Harrison's or Arthur Dyck's reconceptualized view of rights, as *just* (fair) *expectation claims.* See the discussion by Garth Kasimu Baker-Fletcher, *Dirty Hands: Christian Ethics in a Morally Ambiguous World* (Minneapolis: Fortress Press, 2000), 61. Alberto Munera writes, "The concept of need is key to any Catholic economic theory and to any biblical theory of justice. It has no status in global capitalism" ("New Theology on Population, Ecology and Overconsumption from the Catholic Perspective," in Coward and Maguire, eds., *Visions of a New Earth,* 68).

36. A recent study by Women's Voice, a human rights group in Malawi, found that 40 percent of rural women there suffer from domestic violence and other human rights abuses. Organizations like theirs are hampered by lack of funds, transportation, and full-time staff, all of which makes it difficult to expand their work into rural areas (Brian Ligomeka, "Domestic Violence Rampant in Malawi," *Africanews* 55 [October 2000], available

at www.peacelink.it/afrinews.html). For a sobering yet hopeful global overview, see "Human Rights and Political Decision-making," in the United
Nations, *The World's Women, 2000,* 151–76.

37. Cited in David Harvey, *Limits to Capital,* new ed. (London: Verso
Press, 1999), xvi–xvii. The Zapatista movement began as a brief armed
uprising (although its military power is miniscule compared to that of the
Mexican army or of the right-wing paramilitaries). Since that time, Zapatistas have used nonviolent methods. Although I am committed to using
only nonviolent direct action, including civil disobedience, I do think that
armed revolt is morally permissible as a last resort to challenge structural
violence. I came to this view through my reading of liberation theologies.

38. "News and Analysis: April 22–30, 2001," Mexico Solidarity Network, www.mexicosolidarity.org. Pilar Franco, "Indigenous Rights Bill
Recognizes Women's Rights," Inter Press Service, April 27, 2001, and Gin-
ger Thompson, "Added Rights for Indigenous Are Ratified in Mexico,"
New York Times, July 14, 2001.

39. My discussion of these ethical notions is informed by the work of
Sharon Welch; see especially *A Feminist Ethic of Risk,* rev. ed. (Minneapolis:
Fortress Press, 2000). See also the keynote address of Dr. Musimbi Kanyoro
at the 1998 Ecumenical Decade of the Churches in Solidarity with Women
Conference. An excerpt of her speech is in the video of conference highlights,
"Your Story Is Our Story: The Ecumenical Decade and Beyond," available
at www.wcc-coe.org. For a discussion of feminist ethics and public policy,
see Elizabeth M. Bounds, Pamela K. Brubaker, and Mary E. Hobgood,
Welfare Policy: Feminist Critiques (Cleveland: Pilgrim Press, 1999), 12–17.
My understanding of feminist ethics and economic justice was deepened
through my collaboration with Liz and Mary on this volume.

Index

accountability, 75–76, 90–93, 114
agriculture, 48–50, 83
community-supported, 88–89
Alternative Program for the Global Economy, 108–9
Annan, Kofi, 15, 96–97
apparel production, 50–54, 89–91
Appelbaum, Richard, 53–54

Baker-Fletcher, Garth Kasimu, 66
Baker-Fletcher, Karen, 130 n35
banking industry, 21–22, 37, 103
Barber, Benjamin, 101
Barndt, Deborah, 47–48
Barron, Antoineta, 49
basic needs, 32, 87, 114–15
Beck, Ulrich, 16
Bello, Walden, 28, 34–35, 112
Beneria, Lourdes, 113
Benne, Robert, 68–69
Bible, 72–74, 102–3. *See also* scripture
biopiracy, 35
Bonacich, Edna, 53–54
borders, 17–18, 21–22, 95, 100
Border Industrialization Program, 30, 54
Borderlinks, 12, 41, 55, 78
Bordieu, Pierre, 59, 68, 88, 100
boycott, 84–86, 88, 92, 132 n17
Bracero Program, 30, 55
Brecher, Jeremy, 82, 108
Bretton Woods, 24–26

Canada, 47, 49, 104
capital, 18, 21–24, 29, 66, 83, 109
capitalism, 9, 18, 64–65, 70
Chavez, Cesar, 84–86
child labor, 86–87
children, 33, 45, 101–2
China, 22, 33, 53, 58, 105
Christianity, 65, 68–70
class, 60, 66, 72, 84, 100
clothing. *See* apparel production
Code of Conduct, 93–94
colonia, 54, 56–57
colonialism, 35, 68, 107, 124 n56
community, 66, 72, 98, 113–16
Connelly, Patricia, 39–40
consumption, 32, 65–66, 103, 115
conversion, 64, 74–75, 130 n32
Costello, Tim, 83, 108
Cravey, Altha, 55, 60
culture, 17, 65–66, 70

Dakar Declaration, 106
Daly, Mary, 76
Danaher, Kevin, 37–38, 106–7
Dicken, Peter, 19
debt
crisis, 35–37
flows, 22
forgiveness, 101–5
denial and avoidance, 67–68
deregulation, 18, 27–28, 36
development, 23, 25, 29, 40, 83
sustainable, 23, 109–10, 112

economic activity, 20–22
  defined, 113
economic growth, 31, 109, 112
  export-led, 29
  environment, 66–67, 108–9,
    115
  impact of globalization on,
    31–39
epistemology, 76–77
ethic for just and sustainable
  community, 113–19
exchange rate, 25–27
export processing zone, 29–31
exports, 18–20, 35

Fair Labor Association, 94
feminism, 69, 118
Fernandez-Kelly, Patricia, 60–61
*Field Guide to the Global
  Economy,* 17
finance, 21–23
  markets, 110
Fiorenza, Elisabeth Schüssler,
  77–78
food, 8, 45–50. *See also* agriculture
foreign aid, 22–23
Frank, Thomas, 9
free trade. *See* trade
Free Trade Area of the Americas
  (FTAA), 108
Friedman, Harriet, 46, 49
Friedman, Milton, 27
Friedman, Thomas, 9, 17, 29
Fulkerson, Mary McClintock, 65,
  70, 72, 127 n4

gender, 38–40, 60
General Agreement on Tariffs and
  Trade (GATT), 25–26, 38
George, Susan, 21, 27, 32, 33–34,
  42
Global Compact, 96–97

global economy, 17–24
globalization
  defined, 9, 16, 17, 21
  effect on people and the
    environment, 31–42
  history, 24–31
  goods and services, 18–20, 29,
    113
Gorringe, Timothy, 115
Gottlieb, Roger, 66, 67, 70–71,
  79
government, 24, 26, 37
Greider, William, 31, 37, 58
Group of 77, 28
Guatemala, 25–26
Guttal, Shalmali, 32, 38, 106

Harrison, Beverly W., 18, 63,
  78–79, 116
Held, David, 9, 38
Hobgood, Mary, 74
Hodgson, Peter, 72, 77
Huerta, Dolores, 84–85
Human Rights Watch, 53, 86–87
hunger, 45–47, 89

Imhoff, Daniel, 88
imports, 20, 60
International Monetary Fund
  (IMF), 25–27, 33, 37, 102–6,
  110–12
investment
  foreign direct, 21
  portfolio, 21–22
  responsible, 92, 99

Jubilee 2000, 102–6, 113–14
justice, 73, 78–80, 101, 116

Keynes, John Maynard, 27
Korten, David, 23, 31, 115
Kumar-D'Souza, Corinne, 115

labor law, U.S., 52–53, 85–87, 92
lawsuits, 90–92
legislation, 92–94
Lexus and the Olive Tree, The, 9
liberalization, 18, 21, 27–29, 36–37, 102
Lilliput strategy, 83, 98
living wage, 8, 34, 51, 58, 93, 94
Los Angeles, 51, 83–84, 95

Malchow, Bruce, 73–74
maquiladora, 8, 30, 49, 51, 52–56, 60–61
Marcuse, Peter, 17
Margalit, Avishai, 116
market, 9, 16, 18, 89, 109
  free, 27–29
Martinez-Salazar, Egla, 40, 48, 49
McDonald's, 47–48, 59
McGrew, Anthony, 9, 38
Mexico, 8–9, 22, 30–31, 33, 34, 46–49, 53–57
micro-credit, 110–11
migration, 40–41, 49, 83
Mill, John Stuart, 27
Multilateral Agreement on Investments (MAI), 107
Multinational Monitor, 111

National Interfaith Committee for Worker Justice, 98
National Labor Committee, 96
neoliberalism, 16, 27–29
  effects of, 31–42
New Economy, 9
New International Economic Order, 28
Nicaragua, 95–96
North American Free Trade Agreement (NAFTA), 38, 40, 48–49, 117

One Market under God, 9

parables, 72–73
People of Faith Network, 92, 94
pesticides, 48–49, 85–86
poverty, 7–8, 32–35, 46, 103–6, 111, 116
  poor countries, 22–23, 26, 36–37, 45, 102–5
power, 17, 26, 32, 101
  corporate, limiting of, 107–10
privatization, 28–29, 34, 38, 102
production chains, 19–20
property
  intellectual, 25–26, 116
  private, 18

race, 52, 66, 67, 72, 100
resistance, sources of, 70–80
rights
  economic, 114–16
  human, 53, 96–97, 114–17
  worker, 52, 54, 59, 87, 92, 94
Rumscheidt, Barbara, 63, 64, 67–68, 71, 75

Sassen, Saskia, 39–40, 83
scripture, 55, 69, 73, 129 n28. *See also* Bible
Smith, Adam, 18, 27
Smith, Brendan, 108–9
Smith, Dorothy, 121 n7
Social Statement on Economic Life, 80
Solberg, Mary, 76–77
solidarity, 88, 118–19
  sources of, 70–80
speculation, 110
  currency, 23
spirituality of resistance and solidarity, 70–80
Stark, Barbara, 115
Stegemann, Wolfgang, 69–70
Stiglitz, Joseph, 29, 37

structural adjustment program
(SAP), 28, 36–37, 39, 106
sweatshops, 90
in Asia, 57–59
in Mexico, 53–57
in the U.S., 51–53
Sweatshop Watch, 91, 92

Tamez, Elsa, 80
technology, 16, 17, 21, 48, 58
Terrell, Joanne, 77
Thailand, 57–58
theology, 63
of the cross, 76–78
Thistlethwaite, Susan, 72, 77
Tobin Tax, 110–11
Townes, Emilie, 77, 79
trade
free, 18, 27, 33–34
illegal, 19
international, 17–18, 20, 26
Traditional Values Coalition, 64
transnational corporations, 19–
21, 23, 38, 61

Uganda, 7–8, 37, 104
United Nations, 26, 97, 112
Declaration of Human Rights,
96, 114
Human Development Report, 7
United States, 34, 38, 49, 51–53,
61, 104, 115
Border Patrol, 41
Department of Labor, 50, 52
Treasury Department, 28

unions, 27, 38, 51, 60, 94, 95
United Farm Workers (UFW),
84–86

van Drimmelen, Rob, 15, 18, 20,
26
von Hayek, Friedrich, 27

Wal-Mart, 58–59
Wangusa, Hellen, 8
Waring, Marilyn, 113, 135 n25
Washington Consensus, 28, 36,
135 n24
wealth, 7, 23, 32–33, 38, 109,
113, 115
Weisbrot, Mark, 31, 38
Wheeler, Sondra Ely, 74
women, 30, 39–40, 45–46,
51–52, 60–61, 109, 113
*Women, the Environment and
Sustainable Development,* 29
work
casualization of, 59, 88
low-paid, 45, 60
unpaid, 39, 113
Workers Rights Consortium, 94
World Bank, 25–27, 33–34, 101,
102–6, 110
World Council of Churches, 80,
101, 103, 114
World Trade Organization, 25–26,
106, 111–12, 118

Zambia, 36–37
Zapatistas, 78–79, 117–18

Other Books of Interest from the Pilgrim Press

Dismantling Privilege:
An Ethics of Accountability
Mary Elizabeth Hobgood

Offering a solution of political solidarity, Mary Elizabeth Hobgood calls us to look at gender, race, and class as social constructs that suppress some groups and give power to others.

0-8298-1374-8 180 pages, $18.95

The New Job Contract:
Economic Justice in an Age of Insecurity
Barbara Hilkert Andolsen

This is the first feminist analysis to connect religious understandings of economic justice with the issues facing both workers and the wider community. The author encourages all workers to forge solidarity in common concerns.

0-8298-1272-5 164 pages, $15.95

Power, Value, and Conviction:
Theological Ethics in the Postmodern Age
William Schweiker

Schweiker explores responsible ethics, moral formation, and the lives we lead in our complex late-modern cultures. A wealth of material is presented in a unified theological perspective.

0-8298-1297-0 214 pages, $29.95 cloth
0-8298-1290-3 214 pages, $19.95 pb.

The Ultimate Imperative:
An Interpretation of Christian Ethics
Ronald H. Stone

This book is a primer on Christian ethics that offers the reader a fresh application of Christian ethics to the issues that dominate the news: racism, ecology, and the global economy.

0-8298-1330-6 268 pages, $24.95

The Wealth or Health of Nations:
Transforming Capitalism from Within
Carol Johnston

Why has society become so focused on money—and at what human cost? Carol Johnston explores the value assumptions of Western economic theory, revealing what economists contributed and what opportunities were missed as the theory kept narrowing—until only market decisions were considered and money became the only reality. The author offers a proposal to transform the focus of capitalism from wealth to community and national health.

0-8298-1247-4 154 pages, $13.95

Welfare Policy:
Feminist Critiques
The Pilgrim Library of Ethics
Edited by Elizabeth M. Bounds, Pamela K. Brubaker,
and Mary E. Hobgood

A look behind the political-moral mask, offering a theological perspective, and exploring the issues that are at stake for women and children in the welfare debate.

0-8298-1305-5 238 pages, $21.95

To order call 800-537-3394
Fax 216-736-2206
Or visit our Web site at www.pilgrimpress.com
Prices do not include shipping and handling.
Prices subject to change without notice.

THE
PILGRIM
PRESS
Cleveland